# COURAGE TO CHANGE
## THE COUNSELLING PROCESS

*Ursula O'Farrell*

# VERITAS

First published 1999 by
Veritas Publications
7/8 Lower Abbey Street
Dublin 1

ISBN 1 85390 439 2

British Library Cataloguing
in Publication Data.
A catalogue record for
this book is available
from the British Library.

Cover design by Mick O'Farrell
Printed in the Republic of Ireland by Betaprint Ltd, Dublin

*To Carl and Sarah – the most congruent of friends*

# CONTENTS

# INTRODUCTION

Courage is the common coinage between the client and the counsellor. It is never possible to predict the shape of any given counselling session, let alone the outcome of the counselling work, therefore the element of uncertainty and risk is high for both parties. This book looks at both sides in the counselling process. Firstly, it focuses on how the counsellor risks entering into the life of the client, and emphasises the level of respect and unconditional love that is essential in order to do this effectively, without harming either one. Secondly, it highlights the impact on the client of this relationship, and how different conditions and strategies succeed in encouraging her to explore and look at change.

Despite the difference of language and basic philosophies used to describe the various theoretical standpoints, the nature of the actual work may be quite similar within the framework of an open and trusting relationship. The nature of this relationship as advocated by Carl Rogers, and the counsellor-characteristics needed to create the climate within which this relationship can grow and flourish, match my own vision of what is involved. Rogers outlines a way of being and of relating which I would see as the ideal to be aimed at. It is important that those who read this remain aware that the contents depict this ideal, and it is not in any way intended to say that one can only be a counsellor if and when this standard is reached. Indeed to imagine one has reached any such standard would be to suggest that one has 'arrived', and in that moment the work would begin to deteriorate, as the counsellor would have ceased to 'strive' and to grow, and interaction with the client would become automatic and contrived.

The book is divided into three sections. Part I looks at what the counsellor is trying to achieve, the main elements of the relationship within which the work unfolds, and the nature of the close listening on the part of the counsellor, which helps to create and maintain the safety of that relationship.

Part II examines selected sessions with three separate and very different clients. I have tried to illustrate the practical application of the qualities and the listening ability, outlined in Chapters 2 and 3, through close examination of the responses to, and the intuitive acceptance of, the clients' stories, by the counsellor.

Part III focuses on the impact of the work on the counsellor, who is one half of this demanding relationship, and briefly examines the idea that counselling is a creative endeavour, whether long- or short-term. Different methods of furthering the exploratory work, and counselling's relation with medicine, are dealt with in Chapters 8 and 9.

For clarity, I have referred to the counsellor throughout the book as 'She', and I have used 'He' and 'She' for the client in alternate chapters, to avoid the clumsiness of 's/he'.

As an Appendix, I have included the introduction to the *Gloria* film, made in 1965, in which Carl Rogers met with a client for thirty minutes. In his commentary, he succinctly covered the main points of his person-centred approach, and his hopes and wishes for the client, Gloria.

I have emphasised throughout, the idea that counselling is a process, continual and ongoing, and how the qualities essential in order to foster the counselling relationship become a way of being for the counsellor. Our contacts with our clients are brief, in the overall context of their lives, but they are in-depth and intensive, and can have an influence proportionally far greater than the actual time we spend together. It behoves us to proceed warily, with respect and with delicacy. If the client had a voice in this book, it is possible that he or she would echo Yeats: 'Tread softly, because you tread on my dreams'.[1]

1. Yeats, W. B., *The Last Romantic* (London: Arum Press, 1990), p. 25.

# PART I

# CHAPTER 1

## AIMS OF COUNSELLING

*Therapy is not a matter of doing something to the individual... It is instead a matter of freeing him for normal growth and development, of removing obstacles so that he can again move forward.*[1]

### Change of Perspective

Counselling is about change, yet as counsellors, we cannot know what that change will be, or can be, for the client. There will be an element of attempting to free her life from a clutter of tangled experiences and emotions, to try to gain a clearer vision of who she is, and who she would like to be. The effect may not be as dramatic as that suggested by the Zen saying:

> Since my house burned down, I have an uninterrupted view of the moon at night.

but the intention may be similar. She has lost her way, and needs a new vision of where she is going. The aim is not to create a life of 'happy ever after', but to enable the client to find her own reality, her own dreams, and to become free to achieve these. If she is merely trying to fit in with what she perceives as the counsellor's wishes and expectations, then no real change will occur. Freedom of choices, freedom to love and to be loved for being herself, willingness to take responsibility for her actions and to live without fear: the counsellor believes all these can be achieved, not without struggle and pain, but as a result of the counselling work. If, as counsellors, we try to foist on our clients *our* version of truth, whether in respect of themselves, their personal identities, or their view of the world, then we do them a disservice, helping them to create a new mask that reflects merely *our* vision for them.

Feltham suggests that:

> people in difficulty are doing the best they can but often inadvertently dig deeper holes for themselves.[2]

The ability to stand back and actually see what we are doing, to change our perspective of ourselves, is the first step towards planning how we would like to be, and what we would like to do. This can be achieved more effectively with a person who is willing to accompany us on this journey, to focus on areas we are afraid to look at, to accept without judgement the selves we have spent years trying to disguise, and to highlight aspects of ourselves of which we are ashamed. The counsellor cannot do this exploration for us. She has expertise in counselling, but she cannot be an expert in the life of a client. This is reserved for the client herself. The counsellor tries to be the expert:

> ...in making relationships with people, in understanding them, and in facilitating their development in a psychotherapeutic situation in such a way that they become more confident in dealing with their own problems in living.[3]

The assumption is that when the client clarifies what it is she wants to change, then she will find ways, from within her knowledge of herself, of achieving these changes. She will make her own decisions, carry out her own plans, and become empowered to do so as a result of counselling.

Our way of looking at the world and of seeing ourselves within it develops over time, and we become accustomed to viewing our lives in this familiar way, acting out of old habits which may have become complicated and unhelpful as the years have passed. The counsellor tries to help the client to see clearly the patterns she is following, to consider whether this is how she would like to live her life, and if not, to formulate and implement new guidelines and values. The aim is to help the client to discover her real self, and then find the courage to be this self. It is sometimes thought that in order to benefit from counselling, it is essential to have encountered a crisis, or at the very least, to be suffering from so great a distress that, without help, we will collapse totally. But even 'small' difficulties can combine into a situation of unhappy, stressful living, within which we are not coping effectively. And while a life without stress or distress is unattainable, counselling may be helpful towards reaching a tolerable equilibrium.

> It is a serious mistake, therefore, to speak of personality without tensions – to imply, for example, that the healthy mental condition is a blissful absence of tensions. To be sure, tensions which are seriously maladjusted and are therefore stretched to the breaking point do result in mental breakdown. But the thing desired is *adjustment* of tensions, not escaping them.[4]

This recognition of an acceptable level of distress can be a source of great relief to the client, who may have been filled with fears of 'going mad', being odd, being useless. Normalising distress enables the client to be free to explore it and its triggers more calmly, and to focus on the precipitating events as well as on her reactions to them. If clients view a counsellor as an expert with a magic wand, who knows all and will presently reveal all, and who has the power to restore happiness, it is essential that the counsellor does not fall into the position of also believing this fairytale.

...therapists and counsellors who lose sight of common sense altogether, are likely to become arrogant or dangerous practitioners.[5]

It is important that the counsellor does not believe that she is the only refuge, the only person who understands and who can help this person. As well as placing an intolerable burden of responsibility and last-ditch urgency on her, it could also foster a myth of rescuer and saviour. The counsellor happens to be the person available at this particular time, and she does the best she can to help the client help herself. She is not special, she is not all-powerful; she is a fellow human being, a real person in a real relationship.

## Actualising Tendency

When working with people in the process of change, it is essential to have a theory of personality from which to work, and a knowledge of why people behave the way they do. In this book I am writing from the perspective of the Person-Centred Approach (PCA) formulated by Carl Rogers. While it is generally agreed that the relationship between client and counsellor is the key to a positive outcome of the counselling encounter, the form that relationship takes, and how that form is engendered, differs from theory to theory. PCA maintains that the quality of the relationship is more important than any techniques used by the counsellor, and it places the concept of trust at the heart of the relationship.

Rogers maintained that all living things, including human beings, have an actualising tendency, and that given the opportunity and the right conditions, will inexorably proceed to become all that which is in-built in their structure. They will fulfil their potential. If life produced no obstacles to our growth, we would all manifest 'an underlying flow of movement towards constructive fulfilment of (our) inherent possibility'.[6] However, while Rogers' view of human nature is basically optimistic, he did not merely believe that people are 'basically good'. Working within the safe relationship with his clients, he found they expressed anti-social feelings, murderous intentions and bizarre impulses, but that they also tended to 'naturally harmonise into a complex and changing pattern of self-regulation'.[7] From this experience he believed that the basic characteristics of the human being were not destructive nor actively negative, but rather, 'positive, forward-moving, constructive, realistic, trustworthy'.[8]

So fundamental to his theory was this self-actualising tendency, that Rogers believed that while it could be thwarted, it could not be destroyed without the destruction of the organism itself.[9]

## Self-actualisation

Following on from the actualising tendency is self-actualisation, which proceeds with the human being's experiencing of self, an awareness of 'self' as distinct and separate from others. This develops through interactions with others, and leads to a need in the infant for positive regard from significant others in her life. If this need is largely met, then the child's self-image and her real self are closely linked, and actualisation of potential can develop with confidence.

If this need is not met, if positive regard is selective or inconsistent, then conflict and confusion result, with the child constantly anxious and searching for ways of winning some sign of love or approval, and learning ways of behaving which will achieve this. Rather than reflecting on her own experiences, the child builds up a concept of herself to the perceived requirements of significant others. Attempts to juggle incoming information between reality and false interpretations produce tension and anxiety. If the infant perceives some parental response as saying in effect, 'If you do such and such, I will not love you', then the love becomes conditional on this acceptable behaviour. The infant may also hear, 'I will love you if you are good, quiet, smiling, etc.' and begin to build up a self that feels and behaves as she *should*, rather than as she actually does feel and would like to behave. Rogers suggested that this need for positive regard can become more vital to the child than the self-actualising tendency.

Closely connected to this need for positive regard is the need for positive *self*-regard. It is difficult to function successfully if we do not have some ability to feel good about ourselves, and this is hard to achieve if those around us are critical or disapproving. By placing her locus of evaluation in others, and striving to be what she believes others would like her to be, the child's worth becomes conditional on the perceived approval or disapproval of others. 'I am loveable only if I do what is required or expected of me', or rather, 'what I might *imagine* is required and expected of me'. In this way she becomes a victim of 'conditions of worth', imposed by her picture of the requirements of others. She can become crippled by a sense of personal worthlessness, by a total lack of self-regard, and her capacity to feel positive about herself will depend on the quality and consistency of the positive regard of others. Where this is absent, or where it is selective and judgemental, it is difficult to convert it into self-regard. The person, having internalised and adopted the values of others, will have little belief in her own judgement. The measure of her value as a human being, her locus of evaluation, will have become based in others, external rather than internal. She will never feel 'up to the mark'.

### Internal Critic

Thus we develop the internal critic which criticises and judges us from within, undermining our self-worth every day of our lives, constantly finding us wanting. Our real organismic selves are only rarely glimpsed. We present a false self-image to the world, and the gap between this and our *real* selves is ever-widening. The actual experience of the organism is different from that of the self as *perceived*. Authentic living becomes almost impossible, and the individual can become totally split from her organismic roots. She has created for herself a personal version of truth, merely a reflection of how she sees the beliefs of others.

This negative self-image demands that we constantly present a mask to the outer world, that we must constantly try to be something other than our real self. Our inner voice criticises and judges us, replaying previous critical voices, and for those of us with low self-esteem or self-worth, this inner critic can be particularly vicious. It blames us, compares us unfavourably to others, sets impossible standards. It keeps a record of our failures, never of our strengths or achievements. It reads our friends' minds and tells us they think we are boring or stupid. It is so much a part of us that we are often not consciously aware of it. It reinforces our negative self-image and drives our real organismic selves further into hiding, expanding the gap between our real self and our false self-image to intolerable levels.

Sometimes the person can be aware of this gap, this distance from the real organismic self, and can also perceive the lack of unity in this vision of 'self'. Hobson speaks of a 'community of selves',[10] and Rogers concluded that the self is not a fixed entity over time. My self may be visible and capable of being described right now, but a chance remark or happening may change this self totally and instantly. Recognising this, Thorne believes that, 'I am the self which I currently conceptualise myself as being'.[11] My happiness of right now may be misery in an hour's time. It can be a struggle to identify a reliable self-concept, and we make remarks which illustrate the divided nature of our selves: I don't feel myself today; I was beside myself with rage; I don't want anyone to see the real me.

Counselling encourages a knowledge of the inner, real, organismic self, and a willingness to be and to accept the nature of this self, so that the person can acknowledge the use of different facets of self with different people, but remain aware constantly of the inner reality.

The gap that has developed between the real self and the negative self-concept creates dissonance and distress. We are not always aware of this psychological disturbance, because to allow such dangerous sensory experience into consciousness would threaten the self-concept, the picture we must maintain in order to continue to meet the standards of others. Clients often come into counselling with a vague awareness that they are unhappy, that all is not well. When a relationship breaks down, when depression or panic attacks threaten their ability to cope with life, they realise they need help of some kind. The maintenance of the mask or false self is demanding too much effort and energy, and is no longer successful. While the incongruity between real and false self may be below the level of conscious awareness, they are aware of unhappiness, stress and general inability to cope.

Where the organismic self has been almost totally obliterated, and where masks have become the norm, we find a person who is using a script, learned long ago, and playing a role, or several roles, built up over many years. This consists of the picture of how she *should* be, and she has come to believe that the picture is real, and that the script expresses her real self. As the stresses of everyday life increase, so does the energy required to keep at bay the feelings and emotions buried for so long. When this person comes for counselling, her work will consist of sifting through the layers of her false self, which have served her adequately over the years, searching for her real emotional world, trying to discover just what she really *is* feeling, and struggling to identify what values *she* would like to live by. Finding these buried truths is only the first step in her work, because she will then have to choose and plan a new life, reflecting her real self.

## Locus of Evaluation

This person has become so accustomed to accepting the values of others, to allowing others the power of evaluating what she should or should not do, that she is not making clear decisions or choices. She is choosing from a place where she is trying to be as others, in her opinion, think she should be. Her locus of evaluation, the part of her which decides what to do or think, what is right or wrong, is firmly placed in the keeping of others, be they friends, partners, family, religious figures, workmates, or combinations of these. Her life is lived unfree, and every day she strives to meet the perceived expectations of other people, and every day she fails because the imagined standards are unrealistic, and only perfection is acceptable. Her regard for herself is low, because she cannot 'make the grade', and she rarely, if ever, questions that grade. Her levels of guilt and anxiety are high, and her life is a constant struggle.

The work of the person-centred counsellor is to a large extent governed by this locus of evaluation of her client.

> If that locus is markedly externalised the counsellor needs to be aware that the client will be vulnerable to any externally provided ways of defining himself.[12]

It would be foolish, as well as false, to claim that counselling would be the only answer for this client, or to believe that counselling would automatically make it 'better' for her. What can be hoped for is that this client will reach a point of awareness that she is not free, to decide if she wishes to be free, and then to search for ways by which she can begin to make her own choices. To learn to *know* what it is that she herself prizes and values, and to find the courage to make decisions towards achieving these, this is the work of counselling. The time this will take, and the difficulties encountered, depend on the extent of the division between her real organismic self and her public self. Obviously obstacles will arise which prevent a smooth directional curve of actualisation, but clients have an infinite capacity to change, and continually surprise the counsellor both by their tenacity in trying, and their inventiveness in finding new ways of looking at their lives.

## Changing Self-Concept

It would be easy for the counsellor to join the ranks of all the 'others' whom the client is trying to please, and to add her expectations to the client's burden. 'This is what you need to do or to change. Trust me, I'm a counsellor.' If it were so simple, merely a matter of identification of new ways and 'hey presto I'm changed', the client would probably have 'done it' herself long ago. The counsellor is asking that the client begin to be aware, and begin to dismantle this carefully constructed edifice of 'managing' or 'surviving'. To begin to walk after an accident and a year on crutches is not just a matter of physical strength and ability. It requires also an act of faith in my mended bones, the taking of a mental risk, dependent on my renewed image of myself actually walking again. Dave Mearns describes our concept of self, our self-image, thus:

> Self-concept is our *attitude* towards our self. Like any attitude it has three components, commonly referred to as the **cognitive** component (our knowledge and beliefs

about our self); an **affective** component (our feelings and evaluations about our self); and a **behavioural** component (our tendency to behave in ways which reflect our thoughts and feelings about our self).[13]

The idea that there are three components which require to be changed highlights the complex nature of the effort to alter our self-image. What Mearns calls 'an internal consistency' exists, where all the elements are bound together, no one independent of the others, and all together resistant to change. The client may feel negative about herself, but this may be more tolerable and more manageable than the threat of change and the confusion of trying to imagine life without the old uncertainties. A new responsibility for self can be a terrifying idea to contemplate.

The person-centred counsellor, by working with the client rather than advising or taking charge, highlights the dissonance which becomes evident between the real and false self. The willingness on the part of the counsellor to identify and to tolerate this confusion, her acceptance of it as 'normal', renders it possible for the client to tentatively allow the possibility that the real self may not be as ugly, fearful, unloved and unlovable, as she believes. The counsellor offers unconditional positive regard, despite disclosures and perhaps negative reactions from the client, and hopefully she will eventually begin to believe, in small measure at first, that this counsellor may be right. She (the client) may be a person of some little value, who may be a little lovable, and who may be trusted to make small value-judgements on her own behalf. This beginning will lead to an outline of some idea of change, and a wish to achieve it, but the risk-factor is still very great. A client who had steadfastly refused to contemplate a different future life, unable to cast her mind beyond the unhappy familiarity of today, responded with great relief to my suggestion that she *imagine* what she would like to do in the future, without any component of actually doing it. Able to identify her dream in the abstract, she was then able, at a later stage, to consider whether she would make that change or not. Acknowledging the dream to herself, without the compulsion of an accompanying plan of action, clarified for her both the idea and the freedom of choice.

## Altering Behaviour

The fear and reluctance of the client, who is becoming aware of her changing concept of self, demand patience and a large measure of resilience from the counsellor. The natural human instinct is to reassure and to rescue, but this struggle in the client is part of her growth. The counsellor perhaps reaffirms for herself her faith in the process of counselling, her trust in herself and the client and also in her method of working. The next step for the client is to try to change her behaviour in line with her new concept of self because:

> our behaviour is to a large extent an acting-out of the way we actually feel about ourselves and the world we inhabit. In essence, what we do is often a reflection of how we evaluate ourselves, and if we have come to the conclusion that we are inept, worthless and unacceptable, it is more than likely that we shall behave in a way which demonstrates the validity of such an assessment.[14]

It is equally likely that if we have managed to assess ourselves in a more positive light, then our behaviour will in turn reflect this new acceptance of self as worthwhile.

This need to protect the organism from the perceived danger of change is paramount when the client looks at the future.

The skill and professionalism of the counsellor is in not being worn down by the client's protective systems because at this stage that protectiveness is much more in evidence than the actualising tendency.[15]

In the main, the point of change is reached slowly and gradually, with the element of being 'stuck' becoming very familiar both to the client and to the counsellor. At rare times, change can be dramatic, with a startling element of 'eureka!'

> ...the moment of responsibility, when the client suddenly sees clearly that he or she is not chained to the past, or doomed to a particular future.[16]

However it happens, the point of change is rewarding, but it can also be fearful. A client described it as like climbing stairs: 'it's as if I can never go back. Every step behind me dissolves as I take the next step up'.

In an adventure film there was an actor on one side of a ravine, who needed to cross to the other side. He was told there was a bridge across, but neither he nor the audience could see it. In desperation, and with a huge act of faith, he stepped into mid-air and nothingness, to find that there was indeed a transparent glass bridge there to hold him up. Such terror, such risk, followed by relief and a sense of being upheld, can at times be experienced by both client and counsellor at a point of change.

Behavioural change is often slower than cognitive or affective changes of attitude, and the emergence of the 'fully functioning person' described by Rogers, or at least the person on the way towards becoming fully functioning, can be gradual and almost imperceptible, particularly to the client. For Rogers, the 'theoretical end-point'[17] of counselling was a person in the process of achieving self-actualisation, and reaching towards her potential. In her new knowledge of herself, she trusts her experience and her feelings, without being either threatened or defensive, and she is able to live fully in each moment of her life. Her locus of evaluation is within herself, and she is free to make her own choices and decisions, and to take responsibility for these. Rogers was also clear that this state of being fully functioning '…is a process, not a state of being. It is a direction, not a destination'.[18]

There is no cessation of growth and striving, no magic point of transformed perfection. Rogers remained not only clear-headed in his view of human fallibility, but also deeply concerned for, and interested in, what individuals were likely to do.

> …the deeply exciting thing about human beings is that when the individual is inwardly free, he chooses… this process of becoming.[19]

Such freedom can be very threatening for many clients. An awareness of making their own decisions and being responsible for the consequences suggests a strength which many clients do not believe they possess. Having spent a lifetime depending on others, blaming them, or looking to them for approval, it is daunting to contemplate a future where I myself am the last court of appeal, the final arbiter, not only of what I do or think, but of the rightness or wrongness of my decisions. The shifting of responsibility is no longer possible, and I become the leading actor in my own play. It can be exciting, it can be challenging, but it can also be frightening. The counsellor needs to remain aware of this fear, and to remain accepting of possible attempts to retreat, to avoid, even to run away from the new picture of life and living.

The reasons people look for help in counselling are as varied as are people themselves. Some clients come in order to survive, to seek help merely to go on living. Others have become aware that there is more to living than merely existing, and they seek assistance in order to become happier, more fulfilled. We all have a deep need and longing for the unattainable, and we struggle against the certainties of death, of ultimate aloneness, of loss. If such needs become intolerable and begin to dominate our lives, then the resulting stress and pain compel us to look for help. Yalom termed this 'existence pain'[20] because how we cope with these 'givens' of existence determines how effectively we live our lives. One client may fear inevitable death, another may be internally isolated and depressed at the futility of life. 'What is the point?' is a cry for meaning and stability, to which no answer can be offered. Only the client can find her own answer, or acknowledge that there is none for her. The challenge for the counsellor is to sit with the lack of meaning, to tolerate the uncertainty, because these questions also pose difficulties for us as human beings, within ourselves. To remain open to and accepting of our clients, while their unhappiness and hopelessness strike responsive chords within us, is the demand made of the counsellor. And Yalom offers no words of comfort, but insists:

> …the professional posture of disinterested objectivity… is inappropriate…. We are, all of us, in this together.[21]

### Wider Implications

In protest against what he saw as diagnostic and prescriptive approaches to therapy, which confirmed the client's negative view of herself, Rogers laid new emphasis on a relationship based on acceptance and exploration. The counsellor fully trusts the client's ability to know where it hurts, and to find within herself the knowledge of what the solutions are. The potential power in the counselling relationship is easily abused. A client will seek to invest the person of the counsellor with powerful decision-making ability, and a willingness to take responsibility for her. The counsellor recognises what is happening, and is able to refuse and to hand back the power, and to discuss with the client this tendency to yield her power to others. Clients who live in the role of victim may see the counsellor as a terrifying expert, who must be placated and admired. The openness and honesty with which this issue can be discussed enables the client to understand the process, and her own part in it.

The new approach by Rogers, which acknowledged the common humanity and equality of client and counsellor, denied the authority, or authoritarian approach, of the older-style therapist, and vested the power to decide both procedure and outcome, firmly in the hands of the client. The idea of counsellor as expert in the human concerns of the client is one which sits uncomfortably, or not at all, with practitioners of the Person-Centred Approach.

> In many ways person-centred counselling does not fit so-called Western culture… where expertness in the pursuit of authority over others is a goal at every level of societal functioning from commerce through academia to the criminal fraternity.[22]

This same culture is described by Thorne as 'a technological society which thrives on efficiency, quick answers and the role of the expert'.[23]

The counsellor who ultimately trusts in her client's capacity to identify her pain and subsequently to find ways of alleviating it (through exploration in the definable climate of the counselling relationship) has implications for society far beyond the counselling room and the individual client. The idea that people can be trusted to strive towards growth, towards becoming their potential selves, is challenging to even the democratic system within which we live.

> Our educational system, our industrial and military organisations, and many other aspects of our culture take the view that the nature of the individual is such that he cannot be trusted – that he must be guided, instructed, rewarded, punished, and controlled by those who are wiser or higher in status.[24]

Obviously there are areas in our lives where expertise is both essential and appropriate, as for example in teaching, in surgery. But Thorne feels that there are also many situations where expertise is imposed unnecessarily:

> Unfortunately, many of those who have sought my help over the years have spent much of their lives surrounded by people who, with devastating inappropriateness, have appointed themselves experts in the conduct of other people's lives.[25]

Towards the end of his life, Rogers expanded his philosophy and methods beyond their already influential impact on education, industry and social work. He saw the value of facilitating communication between opposing groups, whether religious, racial or political, and he worked with cross-cultural groups in several countries, including Ireland. He believed that the three core conditions, when present in group relationships, facilitated the growth of 'social harmony'. His aim of promoting *real* communication, and therefore wider understanding, follows naturally from his theory of relationship in the counselling setting.

Feltham[26] believed that there are potential connections '...between the listening of the therapists and the potential inherent in a profound political and spiritual listening', and that related group dialogue could have great benefits on discussion and exploration within communities of all kinds, from political, to social, to international. Cultural and religious divides, ethnic and gender differences, are potential barriers to communication, along with differences in value systems, in beliefs, in upbringing. These constitute a personal culture, situated in a wider mainstream geographical culture.

A different language is the great barrier, but even two people speaking the same language with different accents or from a different background, can find it difficult to understand the words and the symbols used.

The use of the core conditions to build relationships makes possible the expression of feelings and attitudes, and the outlining of desired changes. In the final analysis, good counsellors must go beyond the mere imitation of technique to develop their own personal counselling skills, for use in the creative moment. Mearns[27] underlines the 'enormous personal development work which is necessary to win a sufficient degree of self-acceptance which will allow the counsellor to feel consistently unthreatened, accepting and open to the experiencing of her clients', because being a client-centred counsellor demands that we truly become a person who values and accepts, and is interested in, differing clients from differing settings, whether as individuals or as group members. Attempting to understand, and communicating both the genuine desire and the effort to do so, has a powerful effect on cohesive groups and opposing factions alike. The need to be listened to, to be heard and understood, is strong not only in individuals, but in communities also. The focus is on the individual speaking within the group, and the cultural differences take second place to the human similarities.

## REFERENCES

1. Kirschenbaum, H. and Henderson, V. Land (eds), *The Carl Rogers Reader* (London: Constable, 1990), p. 379.
2. Feltham, Colin, *Time-Limited Counselling* (London: Sage, 1997), p. 36.
3. Storr, Anthony, *The Art of Psychotherapy*, 2nd edition (United Kingdom: Butterworth/Heinemann, 1990), p. 28.
4. May, Rollo, *The Art of Counselling*, (London: Condor/Souvenir Press, 1992), p. 49.
5. Feltham, Colin, *What is Counselling?* (London: Sage, 1995), p. 52.
6. Rogers, Carl, *A Way of Being* (Boston: Houghton Mifflin, 1980), p. 117.
7. Kirschenbaum, H. and Henderson, V. Land (eds), op. cit., p. 405.
8. Kirschenbaum, H. and Henderson, V. Land (eds), op. cit., p. 403.
9. Kirschenbaum, H. and Henderson, V. Land (eds), op. cit., p. 380.
10. Hobson, Robert F., *Forms of Feeling: the Heart of Psychotherapy* (London: Tavistock Publishers, 1985), p. 153.
11. Thorne, Brian, *Carl Rogers* (London: Sage, 1992), p. 29.
12. Mearns, Dave, *Developing Person-Centred Counselling* (London: Sage, 1994), p. 38.
13. Ibid., p. 89.
14. Thorne, Brian, *Person-Centred Counselling: Therapeutic and Spiritual Dimensions* (London: Whurr, 1991), p. 169.
15. Mearns, Dave, op. cit., p. 91.
16. Feltham, Colin, *Time-Limited Counselling*, op. cit., p. 25.
17. Kirschenbaum, H. and Henderson, V. Land (eds), op. cit., p. 236.
18. Kirschenbaum, H. and Henderson, V. Land (eds), op. cit., p. 411.
19. Kirschenbaum, H. and Henderson, V. Land (eds), op. cit., p. 420.
20. Yalom, Irving D., 'Love's Executioner', *Penguin Psychology*, 1991, p. 4.
21. Ibid., p. 14.
22. Mearns, Dave, op. cit., p. ix.
23. Ibid., p. 174.
24. Kirschenbaum, H. and Henderson, V. Land (eds), op. cit., Ibid., p. 381.
25. Thorne, Brian, op. cit., p. 168.
26. Feltham, Colin, *What is Counselling?*, op. cit., p. 165.
27. Mearns, Dave, op. cit., p. xi.

# CHAPTER 2

## A HELPING RELATIONSHIP

*I have not found psychotherapy or group experience effective when I have tried to create in another individual something that is not already there; I have found, however, that if I can provide the conditions that allow growth to occur, then this positive directional tendency brings about constructive results.*[1]

It is generally agreed that the relationship between client and counsellor is the key to a positive outcome of the counselling encounter. The form the relationship takes, and how that form is engendered, differs from theory to theory. The Person-Centred Approach of Carl Rogers maintains that the quality of the relationship is more important than any techniques used by the counsellor, and places the concept of trust at the centre of the relationship. Within the interaction, the focus is firmly on the client. For Rogers:

> The whole relationship is composed of the self of the client, the counsellor being depersonalised for purposes of therapy into being 'the client's other self'. It is this warm willingness on the part of the counsellor to lay his own self temporarily aside, in order to enter into the experience of the client, which makes the relationship a completely unique one...[2]

The *person* of the counsellor as an evaluating, needy person is not present. She is neither approving nor disapproving, but accepting of the client as he is, at this moment. The client can face his own uncertainties and threatening truths because such acceptance provides a sense of security, coming as it does without expectations, without criticism, without any sense of fear or threat. 'Unless a therapist can make the patient feel secure, therapy cannot even begin.'[3]

The task of the counsellor is to create the facilitative relationship, but it is not something that the counsellor *does* to the client. It is rather that within this created climate of safety the client can work and explore towards change. This particular relationship demands a large investment by the counsellor of herself. Under everyday conditions, when we meet someone new, we engage in dialogue, seeking to discover something about the other person with which we can identify, some aspect in which we will be interested. In different social settings, we fall in with a set of social rules, or we do not. But the rules are there. At the beginning of counselling, the client is often very unsure, aware of his anxiety and of the dissonance within himself, which have brought him to the point of seeking help. Finding that the 'rules' do not apply, he may see himself in the role of petitioner, or of 'patient'. The counsellor accepts the unease of the client, neither rescues nor judges, but maintains an 'involved detachment'. She is willing to enter into the client's world, divesting herself of her own worries and cares, committing herself emotionally to her client. The client may seek reassurance, and find acceptance.

The client is trying to cope with the current difficulties in his life, and Rogers believed that the type of change required in this instance can be achieved in counselling. 'If I can provide a certain type of relationship, the other person will discover within himself the capacity to use that relationship for growth, and change and personal development will occur.'[4]

By studying recorded client sessions, and then focusing on and analysing those counsellor responses which appeared to produce positive results in the client's progress, Rogers identified three characteristics of this special relationship: empathy, congruence, and non-judgemental positive regard. The growth of the client, and his progress towards change, can be measured in direct proportion to the extent to which the counsellor can offer these conditions. The counsellor needs to *be* these characteristics, so that they become a state of being, part and parcel of the counsellor in her daily living, rather than a set of counselling techniques. However, in the words of Brian Thorne, these core conditions 'are simple to state, more difficult to describe and infinitely more challenging to practise'.[5]

Person-centred counsellors invest themselves fully and freely in this relationship with their clients. This emotional commitment, revealing the humanity, strengths and weaknesses of the counsellor, enables her to enter the client's world. Unlike many other relationships, this special counselling relationship is not fostered through kind words, fine gestures, comforting phonecalls. It depends solely on the core conditions to build up the necessary trust, acceptance and consistency, which create the safe climate within which the client can risk exploration and self-disclosure.

**Empathy or Empathic Understanding**

Empathy is the attempt by the counsellor to enter into the world of the client, often a world of fear, confusion and anger, without the counsellor's own feelings becoming enmeshed with those of the client. It is the attempt to understand the client's perceptual world, from the viewpoint of the client. Rogers defined it in 1957:

> To sense the client's private world as if it were your own, but without ever losing the 'as if' quality – this is empathy, and this seems essential to therapy.[6]

To be caught up into the maelstrom of the client's misery or rage, would mean that the counsellor had lost the ability to be separate, to be secure for the client. Both client and counsellor would be left without a link to the ordinary, and the door between the outer world and the client's inner world would have closed.

The counsellor's persona, her faults, weaknesses, values, is laid aside for the moment, while remaining within her awareness. Her emotional and intellectual sensitivity is focused firmly on the client, and external noises, physical comfort or discomfort, knowledge of time in the session, all retreat to the periphery. Being thus fully open to the client's world does not mean that the counsellor is in a passive state of receiving information and emotional signals from the client. It is an active receptiveness, neither neutral nor invisible, an ongoing attempt to increase her understanding of the client's world.

> ...the therapist senses accurately the feelings and the personal meanings that the client is experiencing and communicates this acceptant understanding to the client.[7]

How this understanding is conveyed, and received, will vary in each relationship. The counsellor uses her body language, facial expression, accepting remarks, constructive reflections, to convey her understanding, because such insightful understanding on the part of the counsellor is of no use unless the client can in some measure be aware of it. The need to be understood is almost as deep a need in the human person as is the need to be loved.

'I know exactly how you feel' is never an acceptable response. We can acknowledge another person's feelings, we can identify similar feelings within ourselves, we can try to sense the unexpressed feelings, but we cannot *know* how anger, sadness, etc. feels for the other. A woman who had been assaulted in the street spoke of her experience to a friend, who responded, 'I was attacked last year and I know exactly how you feel. I was so scared I didn't go out for a week after'. But the first woman said, 'Scared? I didn't think of being scared – I was so angry I tried to kill him. I yelled at him and got in a few good blows before he ran off'.

> It [empathy] is one of the most potent aspects of therapy because it releases, it confirms, it brings even the most frightened client into the human race. If a person can be understood, he or she belongs.[8]

The counsellor tries to express more accurately feelings that the client is unaware of, or barely able to articulate at that time. Clients who have difficulty in focusing on their feelings often lack the words to describe these, rather than actively avoid expression of them. We need to have a good vocabulary of feeling words ourselves, with which to help highlight and express emotional nuances. 'I'm fine' or 'I feel bad' carry neither depth nor conviction, nor convey true meaning, and if we stay with these universal words, progress is unlikely. Mere reflection can also stall progress, as 'You feel bad?' can result in 'Yes. My back hurts'! A more productive response might be, 'This is a bad time for you', 'You're really unhappy', 'I sense you're very miserable', or later in the relationship, 'From what you've been saying, I'm aware life is very tough for you right now. Perhaps you could tell me more about...[some hurt previously mentioned in passing]'. The aim is to restate accurately, more fully, in different words or images, what the client says *and* to add what the counsellor perceives to be just below the client's consciousness.

It is not an attempt to *interpret* what the client has said, or to hazard 'I understand *why* you are angry'. It is to say 'I sense you are angry right now', and hopefully the client will interpret for himself later on. It is an acceptance of the stated feeling, and a tentative expansion of that feeling. 'You say you don't like going to visit her, but am I right in sensing that you may also be afraid to go?' In effect, the counsellor senses and hears reluctance, and risks naming the feeling of fear accompanying the reluctance. This allows the client freedom to be himself, nice or nasty.

The focus is on the client, but we are not looking *at* our clients, trying to measure or size them up. We are, rather, trying to look *with* them at their world as they see it now, and as they explore, we begin to see it with them from a different angle. The empathic understanding is an ongoing process in the relationship between client and counsellor. Becoming aware of the counsellor's acceptance of his feelings, without censure or judgement, the client can then begin to accept them within himself.

Empathy, therefore, is a process of *being with* the client, a way of *being in relation* with the client. Becoming aware of the other person's pain or anger, it can be difficult to sit with these, especially if they are very vivid or intense. The temptation may be to avoid, redirect, change emphasis, rushing ahead because we, the counsellors, cannot bear the pain or the impact of these strongly held feelings. We need to allow the client to acknowledge and experience these feelings at his own pace and in his own time. If the client is attempting to express hitherto buried, hidden feelings, it is helpful to acknowledge and accept the client's difficulty in reaching the point of conflict. 'True listening brings us in touch even with that which is unsaid and unsayable.'[9]

The personal meanings of each and every one of us are vastly different, reflected from experience of large and small events of our lives to date. This is striking when we listen to members of the same family, perhaps close in age, describe their memories and impressions of events, relationships and general atmosphere in their home. At times it is difficult to accept that they came from the same background, shared the same parents. To empathise truly with current feelings and the emotional impact of childhood, and with the client's more recent past, requires the very special listening advocated by Rogers.

## Congruence

The second core condition essential in order to create the safe, secure relationship in counselling is congruence or genuineness, the ability to be truly and really ourselves. We all have some masks or defences, but being congruent demands that the counsellor remain at all times in touch with the flow of her own experience, feelings, thoughts, attitudes, and that she knows how, if, and when to communicate this transparency to the client. Within the relationship, the counsellor is truly herself, without façade or hidden agenda. She does not hide behind a professional role, but enters into the relationship with an honest and sincere simplicity. The feelings, thoughts and reactions of the counsellor must be constantly available to her awareness, to be used in the therapeutic exchange, or placed to one side for future reference, but always available. A measure of the difficult and complicated nature of this second condition is acknowledged by Rogers when he says:

> No one fully achieves this condition, yet the more the therapist is able to listen acceptingly to what is going on within himself… the higher the degree of his congruence.[10]

Other words for congruence are realness and authenticity, and it is often more easily recognised by its absence. When we get a feeling of insincerity or falsity in another person, we will be slow to trust them, and we will be aware that they are masked. 'You don't know where you stand with her', 'He's only saying that to keep me happy', 'Her smile doesn't reach her eyes'. We believe that there is a gap between what this person is experiencing and aware of, and what they are communicating to us. One of the main obstacles to a counsellor being truly congruent can be a fear of others saying, 'You mustn't step out of role, do not be naïve, real professionals do not admit to being afraid or uncertain'. Sometimes it may be sufficient for the counsellor to *imagine* that people could be saying or thinking thus! A counsellor could be afraid of 'losing face', diminishing herself in the eyes of her client, if she were to be truly honest, and she may briefly prevaricate. It is important that she explore (at another time) why she found it necessary to revert to incongruence at the time, with that client. What was the reason for the faltering in being truthful? Is this the way she would like to respond, and if not, why not? If the counsellor is angry with something a client did or said, and reacts unwittingly out of this anger, perhaps by making a sarcastic remark, she may be puzzled by the hurt response or reaction of the client, unable to understand what is happening between them.

> When therapists are not in contact with their own fears, needs, attachments, and aversions, and other unconscious forces, these forces can interfere insidiously with the client's process.[11]

For example, if a client begins a first interview by saying, 'You are the third counsellor I've seen, and it's only fair to tell you that I've a degree in psychology, so I know a lot about this whole area', the effect of this introduction on the counsellor could be, 'The third! That's really putting it up to me. I wonder can I be the one who helps, but that's not likely if others have tried. And a psychologist! I'd better shape up here or he'll catch me out. He must be very clever. He'll know more than me. I must try harder, and be different'.

The reactions range from feeling inadequate, to being impressed by his degree, and include a definite sense of being intimidated. If the counsellor is not fully aware of these feelings, she could react unknowingly with comments such as: 'Third time lucky' (I'm not finally responsible – there's a lot of luck attached); 'Did you learn any special counselling theories when you studied psychology?' (an effort to find out how much he really does know about counselling); 'Right. I usually have good results so I'm sure this will work this time' (a false assurance of success); 'Why do you keep changing? Obviously counselling won't help if you keep running away!' (anger at being put on the spot or being tested prompts the counsellor to accuse the client angrily of running away).

I do not wish to react in this automatic way with my clients, unaware of the reactions within me. If I am finally congruent, I can acknowledge to myself that I am annoyed or intimidated or fearful of being found wanting, by this introduction, and I now have a choice. I can place these feelings to one side (to explore myself later), acknowledge that they are *my* feelings and that I am responsible for them, and perhaps respond: 'It is difficult to find the right person', 'I hope we can work together'. I do not seek to blame the client for how I feel, and I try to understand or guess at his present state. Is *he* intimidated by me, fearful of the whole process of counselling, needing to bolster his own fears by impressing me? Is he defensive, angry, or just rude?

Alternatively I can choose to use my own feelings in an immediate exchange with my client, to help him, and myself, to explore the beginning of the relationship between us right now. I could say, 'I feel quite intimidated when you say that', or 'I feel you're expecting a lot from me'. Either way, my feelings are within my awareness and will not unconsciously sabotage my reactions and responses to my client.

If I make a mistake, or respond in a way I feel is inappropriate, then I believe it is important for the relationship that I acknowledge the mistake or the inappropriate reaction. 'I sense that sounded impatient, and I would like to put it another way. I do not want to hurry you.' Primarily, therefore, the counsellor does not deceive the client as to herself, and within the relationship she is truly herself, a genuine and integrated person, aware of and accepting of herself, not hiding behind a professional mask.

The relationship is obviously different between the counsellor and each client, and the imitation of technique will therefore never suffice. Her way of being with her clients will spring from her *real* self and her *real* reactions to each.

For a trainee counsellor, the dividing line between being congruent and blurting out feelings and reactions can be a narrow one. Congruence is not self-disclosure. Matching current experience to awareness, the counsellor is able to communicate this where necessary, when it is relevant to the relationship and to the work. 'Certainly the aim is not for the therapist to express or talk out his own feelings, but primarily that he should not be deceiving the client as to himself.'[12] The aim is to be transparent, to be open, and not to hide one's real self from the client.

The effect of self-sharing can at times be dramatic, moving the relationship on to a new level. It is risky and it needs to be used judiciously, but where it is timely, it can be most effective. If I fear that not expressing my feelings will result in distraction, leading me to switch away from listening to my client, then it is imperative that I am real in my brief disclosure, and that I bring the focus back to the client as soon as I can. If I believe that a sharing of my present self will enable the client to connect with and express some pain or difficulty of his, then I will use this to strengthen the relationship. The client will hopefully feel safe in responding to the honesty and openness of the counsellor and, as the relationship develops, will be more able to hear what she is saying, and be more confident in her ability to engage with him.

Rogers acknowledged that in the client-counsellor relationship, the counsellor is often faced with the choice of whether or not to communicate what she is experiencing and her awareness of that experience.

> To communicate one's full awareness of the relevant experience is a risk in inter-personal relationships. It seems to me that it is the taking or not taking of this risk which determines whether a given relationship becomes more and more therapeutic or whether it leads in a disintegrative direction.[13]

## Unconditional Positive Regard

Unconditional positive regard is the third condition of the relationship between client and counsellor, which Rogers also described as acceptance, prizing, caring:

> ...a caring which is not possessive, which demands no personal gratification.[14]

The counsellor will accept her clients as they are, and not as she would wish them to be. She accepts all aspects of her clients: their joy, hostility, jealously. The key word is *accepts*, and not approves.

In other words, the caring of the counsellor for the client must be free of 'conditions of worth'. The counsellor needs to convey to the client: 'I accept you as you are, and not on condition that you behave or think in such a way'. She has put aside her judgements or evaluations of the thoughts, feelings and behaviours of the client. The need for acceptance and love in us all is basic, pervasive and persistent, and clients who are defensive, aggressive or vulnerable require this acceptance if they are to discover and to heal their obstacles to self-acceptance.

For a counsellor to be non-judgemental, it is necessary that she be aware of her prejudices and her preconceived opinions, and how she may automatically pass judgement on others before making adequate exploration or enquiry about them. She needs to examine and be fully aware of the values she holds, remembering that they are *her* values, and to be careful not to impose them on someone else, as a measure of her regard and acceptance.

Our values are our moral principles or accepted standards of behaviour, based on our beliefs of what is right and wrong. Counselling can never be fully value-free, because we retain our own values, but we can refrain from expressing these or from using them as measures against which to judge our clients. In this way we allow our clients space and time to discover, or to rediscover, their own standards of how they would like to live. The counsellor strives to prize the person, rather than his adherence to any given standards. For clients who have learned that the love and regard of others is conditional on some behaviour or projected image on their part, this experience of being accepted in counselling, no matter what they do, think or say, is very powerful, enabling them to explore and connect with their inner organismic self, long hidden because it has been perceived as unacceptable to other people. (It is important to stress again that the key word is 'acceptance', not approval.)

The prejudices which the counsellor needs to examine and become aware of in her own life are often based on fear – fear of a group, an idea, a perceived threat to her safety and comfort. For example, if I were prejudiced against people who appear to be aggressive, who talk loudly and stridently, then a client who presents aggressively at the first session could be automatically classified by me as a bully. If I am unaware of this reaction within myself, my responses may be distant, guarded, and aimed at fending off any possible escalation of anger towards me. It will be difficult for me as counsellor to be empathic towards this client, or to enable him to express negative feelings about anyone. I will have prejudged him, and closed him out.

However, if I am aware of this reaction within me, and acknowledge it to myself, I will be able to step beyond it and see that the aggression is not aimed at me (this client does not know me well enough to be personally antagonistic towards me). I will be able to allow for the possibility that this may be an in-built, automatic response to circumstances where an authority figure is seen as posing a threat. My awareness of my own process, of fear leading to a facile classification of this person as a bully, enables me to put aside this inner reaction, and instead help the client explore his response to this meeting. Is there fear or sadness behind this aggressive façade? Is this the response he would like to make in similar situations, and is he aware of the impact on others? I can choose to explain the initial reaction it triggered in me, so that the client can become aware of how others react to him.

The response that would close down any future work would be to meet aggression with aggression. If this occurred, communication, good listening and acceptance would all disappear like snow in sunshine, and the result would be loss all round.

Another example of prejudice might be a counsellor who likes to be precise and to the point, and has little patience for others who are hesitant or who prevaricate. Unaware of her inner dismissal of those who are slower thinkers and talkers, the counsellor might try to hasten the process, filling in words and finishing sentences for him, pushing solutions on a client who has not yet even managed to define the problem. The message heard by the client may be, 'I will accept you if you are concise and to the point, and only if you are concise'. The outcome may be a counsellor who says eventually, 'Well, I helped him to sort himself out, but he couldn't go any further', and a client who returns to his old way of proceeding, more confused than ever.

A counsellor who has identified within herself a wish to be succinct and solution-oriented, an impatience with those less vocal or quick-thinking than herself, can begin to learn greater patience, and to try to focus on the person behind the hesitant words and confused thinking. The client's real reason for seeking help may not be a specific problem, but rather a dimly perceived idea that this slowness is impeding his wish to change his circumstances. If the counsellor is impatient or dismissive, the client's very difficulty can become the block, along with the counsellor's impatience, to solving that difficulty.

## Safety

These three conditions provide the climate and the relationship within which the client can access his inner resources. The existence of these resources formed Rogers' central hypothesis:

> ...the individual has within himself vast resources for self-understanding, for altering his or her self-concept, attitudes, and self-directed behaviour...[15]

Rogers believed that the presence of these three elements in any relationship where the growth of the person is a goal (parent/child, teacher/pupil), can promote growth and change.

> In the emotional warmth of the relationship with the therapist, the client begins to experience a feeling of safety as he finds that whatever attitude he expresses is understood in almost the same way that he perceives it, and is accepted.... In this safe relationship he can perceive for the first time the hostile meaning and purpose of certain aspects of his behaviour....[16]

The emphasis here is on safety, within which the client can begin to take risks of exploration. But the new insights can be threatening for the client, so the counsellor has to be doubly acceptant, firstly of the image of the client which is presented at the beginning, and then too of the person who begins to be revealed as exploration takes place. Slowly the client can begin to accept both his old self and his newly emerging self, because the counsellor is positively caring for him as he was, as he is, and as he is becoming. 'I think the key of therapy is that if people feel safe, they will do anything.'[17]

Self-awareness is not a fourth condition, as is sometimes suggested. It is the means of achieving all three core conditions, underpinning the effectiveness of the counsellor in creating and maintaining the relationship. However, shortly before his death, Rogers appeared to be becoming aware of a fourth core condition, which he described as a hitherto unrecognised spiritual element in the counselling relationship, 'a presence transcending relationship'. When he was closely in touch with his inner, intuitive self, consistently and successfully living the three core conditions in the relationship, then his mere *presence* seemed to be healing and helpful.

> At those moments it seems that my inner spirit has reached out and touched the inner spirit of the other.... I am compelled to believe that I, like many others, have

underestimated the importance of this mystical, spiritual dimension.[18]

It is left to each of us to explore and ponder this fourth element in the relationship for ourselves. Certainly there is much in the special counselling relationship that cannot be captured and reduced to words, that is recognised at a felt level, that only exists in the moment, is glimpsed, and is gone.

## Containment

The counselling relationship is one of respect and equality, with the client's agenda often very different from what the counsellor might envisage for him. The relationship is neither static nor fixed, but rather an ongoing process or progression. The form is fluid and depends on the interweave of exchanges between client and counsellor, like a dance, where the expression of an emotion or a thought by one is followed by a response (in words or gesture or silence) by the other, which in turn dictates or influences the next response. This unstructured quality in the relationship can pose a threat to those who need control and form:

> Indeed, the capacity to tolerate uncertainty is a prerequisite for the profession. …therapists frequently wobble, improvise, and grope for direction. The powerful temptation to achieve certainty through embracing an ideological school and a tight therapeutic system is treacherous: such belief may block the uncertain and spontaneous encounter necessary for effective therapy.[19]

This unique relationship therefore demands that the counsellor lay aside expertise, and enter the relationship without fore-knowledge of either its direction or its outcome. This is acknowledged by those who work in this way, with Casement[20] remarking: 'in every consulting room there ought to be two rather frightened people: the patient and psychoanalyst'. One of the greatest challenges for the person-centred counsellor is to learn to sit with the confusion and the uncertainty of the client and to contain and tolerate the distress and the anxiety. If the counsellor becomes panicked, then the counselling will not only cease to be of help, but it will fuel the client's fears. Without a plan or a compass, she sets out on the client's journey, placing her trust in the client who has no knowledge either of where he is going. She does not hunt for a problem to name and focus on; she does not offer a solution to the initial problem outlined. To be thus willing to sit with, and accept, the client's frightening chaos, can be very difficult, but it is essential if the counsellor truly believes (rather than merely pays lip-service to) the idea that the client will ultimately both identify the distress and discover ways to heal it.

## Trust

If the counsellor is able to embody and portray the core conditions, then her clients will slowly begin to trust her to be present to them, to care, to try to understand, not to judge or to criticise. Patience is needed because those whose trust has been most damaged are those who find this open relationship most difficult. Trusting others has always resulted in betrayal for them, so why should we be different?

The attentive caring and acceptance of the counsellor can challenge both the defences and the self-image of the client. If his self-concept is poor, then trying to cope with the counsellor who positively regards, cares for, loves him, can create dissonance for the client, whose familiar way of coping is being threatened by these unfamiliar attitudes. And here is an even greater need, not only for the core conditions to be present, but for these to be visible to the client. 'It is not enough that these conditions exist in the therapist. They must, to some degree, have been successfully communicated to the client.'[21] A parallel element is where the counsellor trusts her clients. Rogers recognised people's personal responsibility for their own growth and change, and for the direction that growth takes. If we believe that we know best, that people need direction and instruction, that they are not to be trusted to see their own way forward, then we are not working in the person-centred model, which is built on a basic trust in the person. This trust 'is perhaps its sharpest point of difference from most of the institutions in our culture'[22]. Within this counselling relationship, the aim is to release the client's actualising tendency, thus fulfilling his potential to grow towards fuller development. This leads him to accept responsibility for himself, for his feelings, his actions and his decisions, no longer placing his evaluation of himself in others, and no longer helpless. This taking of responsibility leads to self-empowerment and the ability to function in the way he chooses rather than merely reacting to what he thinks others might approve of or accept.

The ideal relationship, therefore, would be one in which the core conditions were offered by the counsellor, in full measure.

> It would mean that the therapist feels this client to be a person of unconditional self-worth: of value no matter what his condition, his behaviour, or his feelings. It would mean that the therapist is genuine, hiding behind no defensive façade, but meeting the client with the feelings which organically he is experiencing. It would mean that the therapist is able to let himself go in understanding this client; that no inner barriers keep him from sensing what it feels like to be the client at each

moment of the relationship; and that he can convey something of his empathic understanding to the client.[23]

As a realist, Rogers always remained aware of the impossibility of achieving perfection in attaining these core conditions, but he did believe that the extent to which the counsellor could help her client was paralleled by her own progress along the road to psychological maturity.

No one of the core conditions can be omitted. They are part of a whole. They become established, not because of what the counsellor *does*, but as a result of the counsellor's attitude towards the client.

And Rogers went further than saying these conditions are necessary. He also believed that they were *sufficient* in the therapeutic work.

> ...when I hold in myself the kind of attitudes I have described, and when the other person can to some degree experience these attitudes, then I believe that change and constructive personal development will *invariably* occur – and I include the word 'invariably' only after long and careful consideration.[24]

Any theory is only as effective as the person who puts it into practice, and because the relationship is central and crucial to the person-centred approach, the personal style of the counsellor coalesces with the theory, and results in a unique way of being, the counsellor living the theory in the relationship. 'Rogers... offers a view of the therapeutic relationship which remains today as radical and disturbing as it did forty years ago.'[25] The person-centred approach indeed demands much of the counsellor.

## REFERENCES

1. Rogers, Carl, *A Way of Being* (Boston: Houghton Mifflin, 1980), p. 120.
2. Rogers, Carl, *Client-Centred Therapy* (London: Constable, 1951), p. 208.
3. Howe, David, *On Being a Client* (London: Sage, 1993), p. 59.
4. Rogers, Carl, *On Becoming a Person* (London: Constable, 1967/1990), p. 33.
5. Thorne, Brian, *Carl Rogers* (London: Sage, 1992), p. 36.
6. Rogers, Carl, *Journal of Consulting Psychology,* vol. 21, No. 2, 1957, pp. 95-103.
7. Kirschenbaum, H. and Henderson, V. Land (eds), *The Carl Rogers Reader* (London: Constable, 1990), p. 136.
8. Rogers, Kohut and Erickson, 'A Personal Perspective on Some Similarities and Differences', *Person-Centred Review* 1 (2), 1986, pp. 125-40.
9. O'Donohue, John, *Anam Čara* (London: Transworld Publishers, 1997), p. 99.
10. Rogers, Carl, *On Becoming a Person,* op. cit., p. 61.
11. Bowen, M. *Person-Centred Review,* 18 November 1986, p. 300.
12. Kirschenbaum, H. and Henderson, V. Land (eds), op. cit., p. 224.
13. Rogers, Carl, *On Becoming a Person,* op. cit., p. 345.
14. Ibid., p. 283.
15. Kirschenbaum, H. and Henderson, V. Land (eds), op. cit., p. 135.
16. Rogers, Carl, *Client-Centred Therapy,* op. cit., p. 41.
17. Corry, Michael, 'Getting the Balance', an interview with Carl Berkely, in *Éisteach,* vol. 2, 5, Summer 1998 (published by the Irish Association for Counselling and Therapy), p. 22.
18. Kirschenbaum, H. and Henderson, V. Land (eds), op. cit., p. 137-8.
19. Yalom, Irving D., 'Love's Executioner', *Penguin Psychology,* 1991 p. 13.
20. Casement, Patrick, *On Learning from the Patient* (London: Routledge, 1985).
21. Rogers, Carl, *On Becoming a Person,* op. cit., p. 284.
22. Kirschenbaum, H. and Henderson, V. Land (eds), op. cit., p. 136.
23. Kirschenbaum, H. and Henderson, V. Land (eds), op. cit., pp. 409-10.
24. Rogers, Carl, *On Becoming a Person,* op. cit., pp. 34-5.
25. Thorne, Brian, *Carl Rogers,* op. cit., p. 36.

# CHAPTER 3

## A LISTENING RELATIONSHIP

*Most of us consist of two separated parts, trying desperately to bring themselves together into an integrated soma, where the distinctions between mind and body, feelings and intellect, would be obliterated.*[1]

### Hearing Beneath the Surface

Effective listening, in the counselling sense, is the ability to hear beyond the words used, and to be aware of nuances of meaning and emotional undertones. It includes a willingness and a caring to make the effort to understand what it is the client is grappling with, what it is she is trying to communicate. The client presents the book of her life within the sessions, brings her whole being, past and present self. The task of the counsellor is to illuminate dark corners and make connections and clarifications which may lead to new perspectives. Often by repeating or highlighting a single word or phrase, the client's understanding is altered.

In the person-centred approach, the counsellor does not have a plan or a map. The only guide is the client, confused, troubled, fearful, who looks at her perceived picture of herself and realises that it is only a surface perception. Accompanied by the counsellor, the client risks looking closer into the picture, to previously unknown depths of emotion, and her picture changes. Like a kaleidoscope, the same pieces are shaken and tossed, and different patterns re-form. The counsellor stays close, trying hard to see each new picture, to understand the confusion engendered by the alteration, and the shape of the new emerging truth.

Effective listening and responding by the counsellor enables the client to risk the exploration of herself, her life and her

53

experience. The counsellor is both companion and creator of boundaries and safety zones, within which the client can take this risk. Clients say, 'I am afraid to cry because I fear I will never stop. I feel I am carrying an ocean of tears'. Or, 'I'm afraid if I allow myself to get angry, I will go berserk and it will take me over altogether'. As in the fairytale, the counsellor holds reality like the end of the piece of string or wool, along which the client can find her way back to her starting point, to safety and to possession of her emotional world.

Rogers spoke of the ongoing process of change in therapy. He described a continuum of change where the client moves from remote and unfelt feelings to owning and experiencing them; from a lack of awareness of experiencing to an ongoing process of experiencing to which she can refer for meaning; from being in a state of incongruence and falseness to being congruent and aware of self without defences or fear, and acceptant of the contradictions within; from being incapable of sharing her real self with others to being both able and willing to communicate herself; from not desiring change to being able to seek change and be responsible for self; from avoiding relationships to seeking them out and welcoming them.[2]

## What is Being Said

Clients usually begin the relationship by telling us their story, where they are currently in their lives, their relationships, and why they have come for counselling. Often they have spent time amassing the courage to come, so when they finally arrive, they allow their tale to spill out unchecked. This is when we hear about their family and friends, their work and their recreation, until the room appears crowded with other people, all closely connected to, and important to, our client. However, if we spend too much time focused on these others, we are merely seeing and hearing our client *in relation*, and not as she is in her own self. By consistently returning our focus to the client, gradually the others begin to fade back into the shadows and our client is free to begin to explore her self.

This is not to suggest that a client is existing in a vacuum, or that we do not consider her social setting, her relationships, her family. But we do need to help our clients to explore (or recover, if lost) their sense of being the actor in their own story, rather than a reactor to the whims and decisions of all the others in their lives. This sense of doing things, rather than of being a person to whom things are done, is most empowering, and brings a sense of decision-making and responsibility for self. The client learns to value her own feelings in a situation, through hearing them being acknowledged and valued by the counsellor.

While we are attempting to see and hear the whole person of our client, we need also to be alert for unusual words or phrases, and the repetition of words used in different contexts. A client came to counselling because she was currently suffering from panic attacks. She described vividly how her throat and her breathing became constricted during these attacks, and she feared she would choke. If she had to make even a small decision she could feel herself spinning out of control, and even her social activities were severely curtailed. Later in the session she spoke about her work and changing jobs, and her feelings of constriction in her new office, as if the walls were closing in on her. The counsellor highlighted her use of the same word, 'constricted', for both situations, and the possible connection between feeling inadequate and under pressure in a new job, and the physical symptoms of panic and fear when called on to make any decision in other settings. Obviously, identifying the connection did not cause the panic attacks to vanish, but being able to understand even a little about why they occurred helped her to be less fearful and to take steps to reduce her stress at work.

Similarly, a client who had developed agoraphobia, several times used the phrase 'dogged by fear' to describe her dread of leaving her house. When the counsellor highlighted the phrase as being an unusual one, without thinking the client replied, 'Yes, I'm terrified of dogs'. It transpired that if she tried to walk to the shop nearest her new home, she had to pass several gates where dogs, large and small, growled and barked and bayed. Underlying anxieties and the loss of her old home, heightened by the animals linking into an old fear, resulted in her new terror about leaving her house.

There are obvious examples as told here, and the wonder is that the clients hadn't made these connections themselves. So often in speaking we say things that we are unaware of, and if a listener repeats them, we may deny that we ever said such a thing. The counsellor is listening with focus and concentration, and often, when she repeats back to a client some word or phrase she has used, the client will emphatically deny saying it.

'You mentioned just now that he makes you uneasy, and I'm wondering what that's about?'
'No he doesn't. Whatever made you think that?'

The temptation to engage in 'Oh yes you did', 'Oh no I didn't' responses, must of course be resisted, and within a few minutes the client may restate her phrase about uneasiness, this time hearing it and owning it, and making no reference to the counsellor's previous statement.

Clients may also make fleeting allusions to important events or emotional states, so fleeting that the counsellor may not be sure that they have been mentioned at all. These elusive comments may spring from the client's difficulty in focusing on such painful or embarrassing material, and she may hope that the counsellor will pick them up and reflect them back, and then they can be examined more closely. Alternatively, they may be subceived, held just below the level of consciousness, and mention of them may appear to be quite accidental. Anne McCaffrey, in her series on the dragons of pern,[3] wrote about dragons that travelled between time and space, and she described their departures as 'blinking out' in the sky. One instant, visible, the next, vanished. Sometimes the threatening or unthinkable aspects of a client's material can blink in and out just as rapidly, and it takes very careful listening to become aware of these, and grasp them for future reference.

## Meanings

Verbal triggers are so personal, and our illustrating images so unique, that it is essential to remain aware that we are all speaking from different experiences and backgrounds: family; school; friends; circumstances. Such a large scale of referents for language and images means that even small variations of meaning or emphasis can distance us from our clients, and can cause complicated misunderstandings. If emotional upheavals further cloud awareness, the gap in understanding between client and counsellor can widen dramatically. The counsellor will try to put aside her own perceptions and experiences of events and emotions, and instead try to link into, and respond to, the experiences and the perceptions of the client. By thus eliminating false echoes and distracting side issues, keeping clear of our own 'interference', we can hope to maintain a clear pathway between our clients and ourselves.

Where we are not clear about the meaning of a word or phrase, it is necessary to look for clarification from our client. 'I'm not sure what *you* mean by "respect" '. So often the reply is very different from our perceived meaning, and if we had not sought clarification, we would have diverged uselessly on our own track. Similarly, if a client speaks indistinctly or through tears, and we fail to hear much of what is obviously an important sharing, it is never wise to pretend we have heard and to continue as if we had. Looking for clarity not only ensures that we get it right, but it also illustrates for the client our effort to understand, the fact that we *are* listening.

If we think of the effort the other person is putting into finding the right words, getting over the embarrassment of sharing hitherto unspoken thoughts, struggling to identify and name feelings which have for so long been repressed and hidden, it is not surprising how difficult it can be for the counsellor to grasp exactly where the client is at, and what she is trying to share. If the client is so unclear and confused within herself, the message being received by the counsellor can be clouded and distorted, and indeed, often requires the skill of a cryptographer!

It is important to try to allow the process to take place, to give space to the client to explore and 'muddle about'. A picture will eventually emerge of the whole person of the client: her feelings, reactions, unhappiness, anger, how she is in this relationship, how open she is to exploring current and past aspects of herself. If we strive too hard to understand and to explore, then we may inadvertently become involved in a struggle with the client, burrowing beneath the surface of the story, focusing too intently on a repeated phrase in order to force its meaning into unambiguous words. Our need for clarity could panic the client through a sense of urgency on our part, where the need to be absolutely clear for the counsellor's satisfaction can become a new burden on the client. The work of therapy is an ongoing process, as the client begins to see herself more clearly in the safe counselling relationship, and begins to venture out from behind the defensive façades to risk and explore herself.

## Personal or Subjective Cultures

Each of us is born into a majority culture, e.g. Irish society, and each of us also has our individual subculture of family, school, church, etc. This subculture is obviously very varied, and is accompanied also by gaps between the individual cultures of client and counsellor. Differences of age, sexual orientation, occupation, gender, marital status, create further obstacles, so the counsellor needs to remain alert to find a common language and expression of feelings, reactions and motives. Even when working with clients from a similar background, the impact of events or relationships can be totally different. This is what renders the phrase 'I know exactly what you mean/how you feel' so inaccurate. I do not, and I can not. It is so much more honest to say, 'I am getting some sense of what you are telling me', 'I'm trying hard to understand something of what it is like for you'.

Fearful clients may have learned to dissimulate for all their lives. We may see their real selves; we may glimpse their hidden selves appearing briefly in different disguises, their personalities flowing into learned roles, each one previously formed in response to how they perceive the demands, preferences and expectations of others. We can find it difficult to maintain our sense of the *real* person behind the flickering and fragmented images. This is part of the dissonance and lack of awareness of self that brings clients to counselling. Our task is to aim for balance and reality, to help the client to recognise, and, if possible, to reduce and learn to cope with this dissonance rather than to solve it or eliminate it altogether.

## What is *Not* Being Said

Listening for the gaps, the omissions, is as important as hearing the content of what the client says. The wish to avoid painful areas of our lives is very natural, and often our clients cannot see a way of introducing the topics they wish to discuss. Perhaps a client who is married spends time outlining her family of origin, her children, neighbours and pets, but her relationship with her husband may be conspicuously absent. Or this relationship may be discussed at length, but no mention of the intimate or sexual side of the relationship may appear for several sessions. It is the task of the counsellor to become aware of these omissions, and perhaps to say, 'I'm aware that you have made no mention of this or that, and I'm wondering if it is difficult for you to talk about this'. So often the relief of the client is palpable as she replies, 'I didn't know how to say it, but you're right'.

More often the counsellor will take note of the ignored subject matter, and hold it in awareness until a connection can be made, or a related comment highlighted. We use the material the client provides – words, silences, tears – in order to facilitate awareness and exploration, to make comparisons and connections, and often to point out what can seem startlingly obvious to us as we listen. This material is usually not deliberately hidden by the client, but is not within her conscious awareness. A client who constantly feels 'not well' and lethargic to the point of spending long hours resting, yet with no symptoms of illness visible to her doctor, may be unconsciously mimicking previous parental behaviour, or her own reaction to her childhood experiences. Perhaps in her home of origin, tiredness and resting were the labels used to avoid stressful situations. Perhaps as a child she felt she could only get attention in a large family when she was sick. Tentative statements about seemingly disconnected events can resonate in the ensuing silence and a client will often make connections for herself, which are more readily owned and absorbed than those offered by someone else.

Clients seeking to introduce a painful topic, not for discussion right now but for the next session, may use the last minutes of a session to introduce a new and important happening or association of ideas. By headlining it in this way, she finds introductory words, alerts the counsellor to a new direction, and ensures that it will eventually be focused on by the counsellor when the time seems right. The difficulty of bringing it up at the next session is diffused, because it has already been mentioned, albeit briefly. Topics or feelings which may appear shocking or unacceptable to the client are often highlighted in this way. Less courage will be needed to continue, if the bare fact has been blurted out as the client left the previous session.

Such 'doorknob' comments may be held in abeyance by the counsellor who, although ready to refer to these during the next session, finds that the client brings new and different material for discussion. Weeks can pass before a linking opportunity presents itself, when the counsellor can make a backward reference to the remark which is relevant to something said today. The counsellor's mind can at times resemble a storehouse of possibly important items, uttered by the client, awaiting constructive communication back to the client!

## Listening to Body Messages

We usually look at a person's face as they tell us a story or speak a loving or an angry message to us. We expect to see there a reflection of the words they are speaking. If we are expressing a message that is *not* matched by what we are truly feeling inside, then we are conscious of the need to school our facial expressions into matching the words we use. A poker face is the attempt not to portray a rising excitement, the blanking of facial expression lest we betray the feelings we wish, for whatever reason, to hide. However, the control often does not extend beyond the face, and clenched hands, tension in the body, a sharp intake of breath, are visible signs of anxiety to the counsellor, even though the client may be unaware of these.

A client who declines to take off her coat, clutching it to her defensively and gripping her handbag tightly on her lap while sitting on the edge of her chair, conveys a visible picture of unease and anxiousness despite protestations of relaxation in the situation. The silence of another client can be interpreted as thoughtful, or hopeless, or angry, by an awareness of her posture: relaxed and still; limp and huddled; tense and on the point of saying something. Turning away from the counsellor or hiding her face suggests inner conflict, which she is not ready to share with the counsellor. It is, of course, only too easy to misinterpret all or any of the client's body communication, but awareness of these potential messages can be helpful in challenging situations. A client who reiterates that she is 'fine', and she just 'wants to chat', can eventually be alerted by the counsellor's awareness of underlying unease. 'You tell me you're at ease, yet I am aware that there appears to be a lot of tension in the way you're sitting right now. Perhaps you're finding it difficult to be here today?'

The need to remain aware of bodily communication includes our own body language, as counsellors. Attentiveness and interest are communicated in our posture, our body angle, and the level of relaxation we convey. (If we are too relaxed, we may appear to be not at all interested, and on the point of sleep!) This 'attending behaviour' indicates our interest in the client, our willingness to be attentive, our wish to hear and to understand. If our body language is at odds with our inner feelings, then this will be readily evident to the client, either consciously or unconsciously. To communicate openly is to be congruent, or genuine.

Verbal, vocal and bodily communication match each other and no real decoding is necessary to understand the message. There is an absence of façade and you feel that you are relating to people as they truly are rather than to their image of how they should be.[4]

The inner calm of the counsellor, which spells safety for the client, must therefore be a real calm, not merely a muffling of fears and tensions. It is essential for the holding and the containment of the client and her potentially destructive emotions, and the client may unconsciously test the ability of the counsellor to survive the intensity of her pain and fury. While counselling demands that the focus remains on the client's pain and tension, the unwary counsellor could absorb this to the point of becoming overwhelmed and overpowered by it. Both client and counsellor could reach a point of exhaustion, where there is no energy left to maintain the thrust of the work. If a client is severely depressed, and the counsellor in turn absorbs this and becomes hopeless and depressed too, then the value of the session could subside into mutual desperation. It is important that the counsellor be aware of this danger, and allow the tension and stress to pass through her, as lightning through a conductor, to dissipate in the passing, rather than to receive, absorb and store it, to the detriment of her work.

## Listening to the Whole Person

> When we are talking about the human being we are talking about two states, the physical state which we can see, and measure, and the invisible state of feelings and emotions.[5]

It is of course not possible to divide neatly one from the other, because the invisible may be the direct cause of the manifest distress of the client. The counsellor remains alert to the whole complex person, aware of the connectedness of the physical, spiritual, emotional and cognitive elements of being. A client who has persuaded herself to act in a manner that runs contrary to her basic beliefs and values, or who has taken a decision to live in circumstances at odds with these, may suffer from stress and unhappiness, unaware of the basic cause of her tension until she becomes alerted to this in counselling. Merely solving problems, even though this is what the client outlined initially as her basic requirement from counselling, will probably not prove effective because the underlying cause may remain unexplored.

Counselling is about helping people who may have problems, rather than offering solutions to those problems. Helping a person to overcome one sign of manifested anxiety may result in the appearance of another. Until the cause of the trouble is identified and recognised, and steps have been taken to come to terms with or to resolve this, then the anxiety will remain. Counselling training explores the invisible state of feelings and emotions but puts less emphasis on spirituality, the spiritual element of the students. It can be put aside as 'religious', unconnected with counselling. In the same way as we learn to be aware of our own value systems, lest they unwittingly intrude on those of our clients, we need also to explore our spiritual values. Whether we are totally committed to, or have angrily moved away from, our religious beliefs, can we allow our clients to explore freely their relationship with God? Can we sit comfortably with one client who spends time exploring the impact of Celtic spirituality on her life, and with another whose deeply spiritual creativity is grounded in an imaginative humanism? If we have no religious beliefs ourselves, can we fully accept and facilitate a deeply religious and conservative client, without pointing out her errors in these enlightened times? Any form of mindset, wherein we believe that we hold a monopoly on knowing what is right or good or 'best', may lead to a nonacceptance of my client's beliefs, or non-beliefs. Lack of tolerance has no place in counselling.

> We need to be clear about our own feelings about spirituality and God. We may have negative feelings about religious institutions and our own religious education which need to be acknowledged.... Psychotherapy and spirituality can meet very well in some ways.[6]

Tolerance, acceptance and non-judgemental positive regard, along with a firm knowledge of our own beliefs and an equally firm resolve not to impose these on others, will enable us to be fully with our client in freedom.

## Transferred Feelings

Central to the relationship in many theories is the concept of transference, where new editions or reprints of psychological experiences are transferred on to the therapist. Rogers believed that feelings and emotions towards the counsellor could be a direct response, positive or negative, to the behaviour or attitude of the counsellor. The client might be relieved and thankful at being understood and accepted, or angry at being apparently misunderstood, and may respond with warmth or resentment towards the counsellor's own person and actions.

Alternatively, the client's emotional reaction may bear little relationship to the actual behaviour of the counsellor, but may be transferred on to the counsellor from within the client. These reactions can also be positive or negative, and are projected from their true origins, towards a significant person in the client's life, often a parent.

Or, and this is less often recognised, they can be negative

attitudes towards the self, which the client cannot bear to face. In the therapeutic interaction, all of these attitudes – positive or negative, 'transference' feelings or therapist-caused reactions – are best dealt with in the same way.[7]

In the person-centred approach, therefore, *all* feelings, including transferred feelings, can be explored. The counsellor may be loved for what makes her loveable, disliked for what makes her unlikeable, or she may receive *transferred* love or dislike. If there are feelings in the relationship that owe their origin to the client's childhood, then these are acknowledged and explored in the moment, not dealt with differently. Within the counselling relationship, the client can explore and relive all her other relationships: herself as child, wife, mother, etc.

Indeed, Rogers stated that 'to deal with transference feelings as a very special part of therapy, making their handling the very core of therapy, is to my mind a grave mistake'[8]. Rogers was not condemning the idea or the possibility of 'transference'. He deplored its use as the 'very core' of therapy.

Where a client's feelings are directed towards the counsellor, it is important (but not always possible) that the counsellor be aware of her own response. Remaining focused on the person of the client, recognising and assisting the exploration and expression of anger by the client, the counsellor does not respond from the anger within herself. To do so could invite a shouting match, where anger meets anger, sparks fly, and communication and understanding disappear. The fully functioning counsellor will become aware of the impact the client is having on her, and will acknowledge that the client is 'pressing her buttons' and that she is becoming angry in a predictable fashion. This acknowledgement and acceptance of her own positive or negative feelings enables the counsellor to respond openly, perhaps by saying: 'I really feel angry when you say I am lying. I'm not sure if you really believe that, but I feel I don't fully understand what's happening between us right now'.

This kind of openness and honesty on the part of the counsellor can often create a turning-point in the work, encouraging the client to be courageously honest in turn. The impact of the client on the conscious or unconscious feelings of the counsellor is termed counter-transference. It is important in the therapeutic work that the counsellor remain always aware that she is totally involved in this relationship, and that such involvement means that she does not move unscathed and untouched through a session. Constantly re-examining the impact of the relationship on her self, and constant interaction with her supervisor, enables the counsellor to be open to an awareness that clients involve us and influence us, and we are not always aware of this in the moment.

## Obstacles to Effective Listening

Obstacles and distractions to good listening include those from within ourselves, conscious and unconscious, and those of the circumstances within which we are working. Our clients can also at times seek to distract us from the painful material that is about to surface, or has already been mentioned, and the counsellor can be seduced into a discussion of Church or politics, new books or films, colluding in the client's avoidance. Distractions from the tangible world around us include the room being too hot or too cold, uncomfortable chairs, noises and sounds such as phones, ambulance sirens, raised voices, children playing – any distracting sights or sounds. I once worked with a client who sat with her back to a window, through which I could see lightning and rain as a severe storm blew up and tore through the garden outside. My client was oblivious of anything other than the unhappiness she was caught in, but I was distracted to the point of being about to apologise for my attention straying, when a violent thunder clap broke through her concentration! Acknowledging our distraction at such times is wiser and more congruent than maintaining a façade of listening, while our attention is elsewhere.

If the counsellor is tired or worried about her own affairs, this anxiety can create a false picture of attention for the client when the counsellor is actually focused firmly on her own self. Half listening is potentially more dangerous to the relationship than not listening at all or mentioning our distractions to the client. By pretending to have listened closely to what our client is saying, we may miss an important part of her story, our responses will be either stilted or inaccurate, and our lack of congruence at that time may do irreparable harm to the relationship and the atmosphere of trust.

Being over-eager to help, or focusing on the problems presented by our client and on our attempt or determination to solve these, can also serve as a distraction to true listening. Clients who are unsure of their feelings, inexperienced at identifying these, or reluctant to name them, can seek to present us with a labelled problem as defence against the threatening feelings. If we stay with this focus, then we may feel satisfied that we have 'solved her problems', but in fact we will not have truly heard the underlying cry for help to explore and to learn how to cope, from the client's inner life of pain and fear.

Prejudging a client, or her material, can result in our hearing what we *expect* to hear. Working with a young person we have pre-labelled 'difficult' could result in our listening in such a way that we filter all the facts and feeling-statements through the sieve of the idea of 'difficult'. Indeed, this filtering can be equally inaccurate in a positive sense, when we listen to a client, for example, who comes from our own county or who attended our old school. This can result in a kind of halo effect, where the client's material is coloured and slanted and heard through our imagined fellow-feeling for someone we believe has come from the same culture or experience as ourselves.

Written notes from a referring source can have a similar effect, again positive or negative, outlining the person's difficulties from the perspective of a third person.

The quality of our listening and our hearing can also be altered by the introduction, by the client, of information and comment on many other people, perhaps relations, children, family of origin, workmates. This diffusion of attention, as we try to identify, name and remember the client's whole social circle, can materially affect our true hearing of the client's personal difficulties. By focusing attention on the client herself, and trying to listen to the impact of the various people on her rather than retain details of *their* lives, we ensure that we are listening to, and hearing, what the client is trying to say to us.

The client and the counsellor often have different agendas, about both the pace and the direction of the work, as well as about the desired results.

My agenda for my client is that *her* hopes and dreams will come true, and that she will achieve whatever is fully functioning for her. She is painting this picture – not me.

The client may be apprehensive and may try to invest a large degree of power in the person of the counsellor. The counsellor will not accept this position of authority, for to do so, unwittingly or otherwise, can result in the abuse of the powerlessness of the client. By constantly remaining aware of the responsibility of the client for herself, the counsellor enables the client to become empowered. A client of long standing once told me:

> I believed for ages that you knew all the answers, and that if I sat for long enough and worked hard enough, I would reach the solutions I knew you had all the time. That kept me going, even when it felt hopeless. It was quite shocking to realise one day, from something you said, that you didn't know the outcome either. I was terrified, but I suppose there was an element of pride there too – it was up to me to make it, and I wasn't alone.

The client may come hoping to meet an advice-giver and problem-solver; a father- or mother-figure to protect and take responsibility for her; an extension of authority like a teacher or a director; a power figure, a nurturer, a friend. These expectations may be positive or negative, but the beginning of the counselling work may be fraught with the realisation that this relationship is not only not going to meet expectations, but is not like any other known relationship.

This focused and totally attentive listening is difficult to achieve, and is rarely met outside the counsellor's sessions. It is indeed a most potent force for change, enabling a client to hear herself through the medium of the counsellor, recognising herself in the accurate reflection by the counsellor of what she has heard beyond the words and current limited understanding of the person seeking help.

# REFERENCES

1. Kirschenbaum, H. and Henderson, V. Land (eds), *The Carl Rogers Reader* (London: Constable, 1990), p. 370.
2. Kirschenbaum, H. and Henderson, V. Land (eds), op. cit., pp. 412-16.
3. McCaffrey, Anne, *The Dragons of Pern* (London: Sphere Books Ltd., 1974).
4. Nelson-Jones, Richard, *Practical Counselling Skills* (United Kingdom: Holt, Rinehart and Winston, 1983), p.25.
5. Corry, Michael, 'Getting the Balance' in *Éisteach,* vol. 2, 5, Summer 1998 (published by the Irish Association for Counselling and Therapy), p. 22.
6. O'Floinn, Caoimhe, 'Women's Spirituality and Psychotherapy' in *Éisteach,* vol. 2, 8, Spring 1999, pp. 4-5.
7. Kirschenbaum, H. and Henderson, V. Land (eds), op. cit., pp. 130.
8. Kirschenbaum, H. and Henderson, V. Land (eds), op. cit., pp. 134.

# PART II

# INTRODUCTION

In the following 'practical' chapters I have illustrated three different clients, in very differing circumstances. Their expectations of counselling varied, and the length of time they each spent in counselling appeared to be the time needed to fulfil these expectations, which were often different from mine. I have set out details from six sessions with each client, sessions which I feel illustrate the nature of our work together. In my work generally, and in the outlines here, I have used ideas and examples from my supervision sessions with students over the last number of years. I would like to thank these students, whose willingness to risk and to share with me their experiences with clients, and aspects of their interactions, has contributed so much to my learning, and to my own work with clients.

I hope these sessions will illustrate different ways of applying the core conditions outlined by Carl Rogers. If we *live* these conditions, our interactions with our clients will be illustrative of them.

> ...it is fair to state that the person-centred counsellor must learn to wear her expertise as an invisible garment if she is to become an effective counsellor.[1]

As the work progresses the counsellor may be seen as 'abdicating power in order to empower',[2] and the troubled picture of the client and how he sees change can alter dramatically. Clients need time to process what arises in the sessions, to absorb and ponder on what resulted from their explorations. Sessions therefore usually take place once a week, and last for an hour. This appears to be the optimal time for concentration and productive attention. It is essential that counsellors remain aware that they only see a client for one hour a week, and that the intervening time is spent in the client's own social, family, internal world, perhaps thinking and reassessing what they discussed in the session, but also dealing with the distractions of living their lives. Looking at current events and reactions often highlights familiar feelings from a client's earlier life. It can be valuable to examine and re-experience these, not with any foolish notion of changing that past, but because our childhood casts long shadows. Ivor Browne put it succinctly:

> What has happened has happened. We are not dealing with the past, but with the effects of that past upon the present.[3]

It is impossible to convey fully what happens in a counselling session. What does the counsellor do, and what does the client do? The moment-to-moment nature of the interaction, the fact that so much of the session is concerned with feelings, not with details or ideas, the fact that many people process their lives in images rather than in words, the intangible nature of the relationship which underpins the work, can only be hinted at in the written account. The words describe merely the words, and omit the feelings, the colours, the sense of closeness, of discovery, the pain and the struggle. Each session begins and is completed, totally unique and never to be repeated, a stepping stone in the client's life (and in the counsellor's experience) which shimmers briefly and vanishes, like a disturbance on the surface of a lake. It happened, the ripples spread, and then it is gone.

#### REFERENCES

1.  Mearns and Thorne, *Person-Centred Counselling in Action* (London: Sage, 1988), p. 6.
2.  Ibid., p. 18.
3.  Browne, Ivor, *Sunday Business Post*, Dublin, 11 July 1999, p. 17.

# CHAPTER 4

*I am trying to determine whether my understanding of the client's inner world is correct – whether I am seeing it as he or she is experiencing it at this moment.*[1]

## CLIENT ONE: JOAN

Getting ready to see a client for a first session can be a time of tension and worry. What is this client going to be like? Will I be able to help? Will I be able to stay with the client, no matter how awful her story? Will I meet his expectations? While it is not comfortable, this tension is indicative of being neither complacent nor casual in our approach, and of our openness and willingness to accept this client as she or he is. If we reach a stage when we await a new client with the attitude of, 'So what? It's just another client', then we run the risk of seeing the client as a cypher, an insubstantial shadow, who will not really impinge on us as persons.

### Session 1

Joan contacted me through a centre where I once worked, and arranged an appointment on the phone. She told me that she was a single mother and that she wanted to discuss her current situation, that she needed help in making some important decisions in her life. She came on time, settled herself in a composed way, appearing neither anxious nor at ease. She was tidy in her movements, and I sensed a containment that was taut and controlled. She spoke quietly, unemotionally, flatly, and told me she was twenty-eight years of age, living on her own in a flat with her son Seán, aged three, and that she had been separated from the boy's father, Declan. Declan had been away for nearly four years but had recently returned, and he had contacted her to say that he wished to see his son and gain visiting rights with the boy.

'I lived with Declan for two years and we got on OK, but he walked out when I became pregnant. I had to go back home, but now I've my own flat and Seán and I are together and that's all that matters. Declan rang out of the blue last month and said he wanted to come back into our lives in some way, and that he wanted to get to know Seán, that as his father he has some rights.'

I was aware of the deadpan tone of her voice, and the phrase 'got on OK' had sounded very lukewarm. If she was in any way contemplating renewing the relationship with Declan, it would be important that she remember it as it had been.

'You say he wants to reconnect, and that before he left, your relationship was "OK"?'

'Well… he was fine when he wasn't drinking. But he was drinking more and more.'

A note of revulsion, or fear, in her voice prompted me to say 'You didn't like his drinking?'

'He used to get quite violent – noisy first, then violent, smashing things and slamming doors. He only hit me once, and I left for a week. I had to stay out of work because I'd bruises on my face. I went home, but my mother said he'd probably never do it again, and it was only the drink talking.'

Although I am aware that the quiet voice is lacking in emotion, and that Joan is speaking as if merely reading a story, it is too soon to focus on and highlight underlying feelings. If she has created a gap or a split between story and emotions, then eventually it will be essential for her to reconnect with her feeling self, but our relationship is too new to support or survive probing.

There was a long pause, and then Joan said:

'I wish I hadn't listened to her and never gone back. Then it would be different now.'

And after a further pause:

'I really never want to see him again, but fathers are important, aren't they? Do you think so?'

I sense Joan might like to hear me say, 'No, not that important', and then the 'expert' would have indicated that there was no real need to be in contact with Declan again. Instead I said:

'They appear to be important to you.'

Just for a moment I thought Joan was going to disclose her own ideas about fatherhood, but instead she checked herself, and said:

'That's why I cannot make up my mind about letting Declan meet Seán. I don't know what to do.'

It is sometimes suggested that the first session with a client contains the seeds of all future work, if the counsellor can pick these up. Joan's comment about fathers being important, offered as if there were a doubt in her mind as to whether they *really* mattered, was probably an issue to which she would return. Just now it is too soon for her to explore with me her relationship with her own father, his place in her family of origin, or indeed if he had been present at all during her childhood.

'I'm hoping you can help me decide. I've read a lot about how important it is for a child to have two parents, and especially for a little boy to have a male role-model, but I just thought he'd have to do without, as if Declan was dead, because he just disappeared. And now he's back and I have to face up to the whole situation again.'

I decided not to be drawn into a discussion about good parenting, as underneath her worries as a parent, I sensed that Joan felt catapulted into an old situation, which she had painfully come to terms with over the four years. She hadn't planned this, and was perhaps feeling helpless in the face of this sudden reappearance and demand.

'It must have been a great shock for you to hear from him after so long.'

'Shock? I nearly passed away. No one had warned me he was coming back, just this voice on the phone. It was like an earthquake, I thought I'd die. And no "Sorry, how are you?" Just "Here I am" and "When can I see Seán?" I don't even know how he knows his name. I suppose his brother told him, he's in touch with my cousin.'

I can hear shock tempered with rage in Joan's voice, and she describes Declan's leaving after she told him she was pregnant, and how she'd had to face her pregnancy and the birth without him. She spoke with pride of how she'd managed with the small baby, with the help of friends rather than family, and how Declan's family had followed his lead and had not wanted to know about the baby. Our hour was now ended and I suggested we arrange to meet for six sessions and then see how the work was going. We could re-contract at that point if she wished. Joan agreed appointment times: 'Because I've got to get this sorted. He said he'd ring me again next week'.

I now know some of Joan's story, and I'm aware of her love for her little boy, her anxiety to do the best she can for him, her anger against Declan, possible helplessness in the face of this new situation, and also lack of support from both families of origin. I see that I must be careful not to become entangled in my own impulse to protect a small child, and in my own feelings and values around a man who left her when she was pregnant. If I indulge these in myself, I will not be able to help Joan explore effectively *her* reactions to this demand, and her ability to make a responsible decision about the future.

## Session 2

Joan arrived on time, more agitated (and more alive) than in the first session. She launched immediately into, 'He was on the phone again – pushing me. And my mother has heard – I didn't tell her – and she says it's great, and will we be getting married? She hasn't a notion. Just to have a man, almost any man, that's all she thinks is important. She's always been the same'.

'I sense you don't agree with her?'

'Of course not. They're all the same. Sex and drink – drink and sex. And never there when you want them.'

I am aware that Joan's rage is as much against all men as against Declan himself, so I say, 'You sound quite bitter about men in general'.

As I said this, I disliked the word *bitter*. 'Scornful' would have been less threatening and perhaps also more accurate. I also thought, on reflection, it would have been more effective to have retained the focus on Declan. However, Joan continued as if I'd said nothing.

'I remember at school, there was a teacher, we had him for art. He was old and ugly, and had hands all over the place, but none of the others really minded. I hated him, and the others used to tease me about being his pet. I wasn't able to stand up for myself I suppose, so I always got picked on.'

I had a sense of a lonely little girl, isolated and perhaps even bullied at school. Joan had abruptly shifted from anger to sadness, and sadness can be more 'acceptable' and often easier to tap into and express. I was tempted to try to re-focus her on her anger, but decided to stay with her in the moment. I reflected back, 'You're feeling sad just thinking about it'.

It seemed important to focus on this feeling of sadness, rather than to question her about the events of school life. These would emerge later, if they were important, and if she stayed with the sadness.

There was a long silence as Joan struggled not to cry. Finally she succeeded in saying:

'If I get caught up in tears, I'll lose sight of what I'm trying to decide. I have to be strong for Seán, and tears are useless. What's the point in crying? People only look on you as weak, and take advantage and push you around'.

Joan almost allowed her unhappiness to emerge, but decided instead to remain 'strong', and turned away from her inner sad self. I would have liked to focus back strongly on my recognition of this sadness, but in these circumstances I felt it would be inappropriate, as Joan has highlighted being bullied and being pushed around. I do not want to join those who have bullied her, so I choose instead to hold both the image of deep and concealed misery, and Joan's idea of strength as being unemotional. I am also aware that this is only our second session, and that it is too early for me to know how strong Joan's defences are, and how important they are for her survival.

After another pause, Joan said:

'I don't know why I remember this, but my brother (he was three years older than me) always used to be at me, and breaking up my things. I remember a doll I had, Susie, with blonde pigtails and a red dress. I got her for my fourth birthday, and I only had her for about a week (it's amazing how well I remember her) when Tony got mad one day over something, and just pulled her to pieces. It was in the yard so no one came, and when I collected the pieces and brought them into Mam roaring crying, she just said I must have annoyed him, and she'd get me another, and she put all the pieces into the stove. I don't remember getting another doll, and I just knew he'd always win, so it was no use fighting him.'

I felt so angry for the little girl, who had learned not to cry and to 'tough it out', but I was also aware that if I allowed *my* rage, or my deep sympathy, to pour out, it would damage my impartiality and my ability to listen to and stay with Joan's recall and re-experiencing of *her* emotions, and it might also impede Joan's own deep feelings. Was she sad, angry, filled with hatred, resentful, afraid, helpless?

To name any one of these feelings might induce in Joan a sense of 'this is what I ought to feel, because this counsellor, this expert, believes this is right'. If this happened, once again Joan would be focusing on what other people thought she 'should' do or be, rather than on her own real and true feelings, the reactions of her organismic self, which she appeared to have buried deeply.

However, I acknowledged to myself how I was feeling, and Joan herself answered my query without being asked.

'I was terrified of him, and Mam always took his side. She always said don't let them know, just carry on as if it didn't matter, and then they get no satisfaction.'

I wondered if Joan's decisions about visiting rights were being made more difficult by her fears of Declan hurting little Seán as her brother 'hurt' her doll. I felt it was too soon to share this idea, but it was important that Joan acknowledge the fear, which may be beneath the anger, neither of which feelings she knows how to express.

'I sense you may be frightened of Declan in the same way?'

The silence here was so long that I was afraid I had said the wrong thing, that I was way off the mark, and even that Joan had withdrawn from me altogether. I hoped that she was considering the validity of what I had offered, if it felt 'right' for her inside, so I sat with the silence, and waited.

'I really feel frightened of everyone, except Seán. They expect so much of me, always wanting me to do this, be that. They haven't a clue about what I'm really like, how scared I am. And I don't like saying that even, because if I allow myself to be scared, how will I ever do anything?'

'You're really afraid of being afraid?'

And here Joan did weep, long and painfully, allowing herself to acknowledge and stay with her very real fears.

As our time was almost up, Joan spent the next ten minutes regaining her composure and putting on her 'public' face to face the world. Surprisingly, she was not devastated as I had feared, but more relieved, as if she had looked at her inner self, allowed it to emerge briefly for her own scrutiny, and in some way now she had less of it to pack away again. There was a sense of relief and a new awareness, which she said she would look at over the next week, before her next session.

## Session 3

In the third session, Joan was wary and watchful, uncomfortable that she had 'broken down' during the last session, and determined that this time she wouldn't be 'weak'. She actually said, 'I don't know what got into me last time. I expect I wasn't feeling great after the flu. I haven't cried for years'. It often happens that after an intense session, where feelings have been named and expressed perhaps for the first time in years, a client will cancel the following session, or come determined to be 'stronger'.

It is important that the counsellor register the sequence, as it is often indicative of the fear of the client at expressing strong feelings. Whether to mention it at the time or not is a choice the counsellor will take in each different case. Sometimes it is good to mention or recognise the intensity, 'I'm aware that last week was a very difficult session for you', without actually making what could be an accusatory connection, such as 'You should have come no matter how hard the last session was'. It may be more useful in the work to highlight this later on, when the client may be ready to hear the possibility that this is a pattern that she uses in her everyday life (unconscious avoidance after an emotional event) and one that she may wish to change on becoming aware of it.

'I really need to make up my mind about letting Declan see Seán. Perhaps if I tell you the background, you will be able to tell me what to do. I don't want to, but I don't really think I have any choice.'

Joan talked about her need to find out what was the legal position regarding Declan and Seán, so that she would be armed with this information if Declan tried to talk her down. I explained that I didn't have this information, but I gave her the name and phone number of an organisation that supplies free legal information for women.

'If he wants one thing, and I hold out for something else, I'll find it very hard to stand my ground. I always seem to give in to people telling me what to do, so I need to have it all planned out.'

Joan was genuinely afraid that she'd give her power to Declan and give in to whatever he asked. She had little awareness or recognition of her inner strength that had helped her to fight to keep her child and manage effectively so far. Rather than help her to plan and have everything under strict control, I reflected back to her my impression of her.

'I imagine you've managed many difficult situations over the past few years, planned and unplanned.'

She seemed genuinely astonished by this idea, but said:

'Well, I'm well able to speak up when it's about Seán. No one is going to push him around if I can help it.'

I waited to see if she would hear the discrepancy here between 'I always seem to give in…' and 'I'm well able to speak up…', and after a few minutes' silence, she did.

'It's different when I'm defending someone else. It's as if *I* don't feel I have any rights. I remember at home my mother was always saying, "Here's your father. Get up and get his tea, give him your seat, put out the dog". I might be tired or sick, but when he came in, all attention had to be paid to him. It was as if she and I were skivvies. I remember her creeping around the house a lot, quietly, as if she didn't belong there, as if she were on trial. And I had to do the same, but I'd be raging inside. And whenever I broke out, and was late home or too noisy, it was as if I was hurting or harming her. She needed me to be mouse-like too.'

Here Joan sat gazing into the distant past, reliving some of her childhood, trying to see how it had been and how it was affecting her now. After a long silence:

'I feel as if I've lived in a tight box, squashing myself into someone else's shape. I'd love to escape and go wild, and shout and dance, and tell them all where to go. I used to love Irish dancing, and now when I see *Riverdance*, I'd love to do that.'

Joan's voice was energised and alive, and I saw a glimpse of the small child she'd been, full of joy and excitement. This quickly faded, and she returned again to the controlled and tight self she'd learned to be.

'I suppose I'll have to say yes to Declan. Seán has been asking too, and he says the boys at playschool say he has no father. But I can't bear the thought of him coming to the flat. That's mine, and if he's been there, it will be different.'

As our time ended, I said:

'I'm aware that the whole situation is bringing back a lot of old memories and that it is difficult for you in more ways than one. It isn't just a simple matter of visiting rights. It's much more complicated.'

Joan seemed relieved that I could see some of the complications. I highlighted her choice in this matter, that the decision would be hers in the end. 'It is a hard choice, and perhaps you could begin with a smaller choice, perhaps to decide that you will give Declan an answer in a month's time. That might take some of the pressure off the decision, and give you a better chance to find out what you'd like to do?'

This was directive but I felt she needed some space to make up her mind, and she wouldn't have this if he was ringing her every few days, and she was trying to go on saying 'not yet, not yet'. Focusing on a lesser decision to start with can be empowering, and can dilute the intensity around a single decision point. Joan thought she might try this, and I was glad she hadn't whole-heartedly agreed. My role as perceived 'expert' and advisor was lessening.

## Session 4

When Joan arrived for her fourth session, she was obviously very angry, with her eyes literally 'flashing'. She had hardly sat down when she burst out:

'That so and so! He was around visiting Mam, asking her when she saw Seán and telling her I was being "difficult". Difficult! And Mam is taking his side, and telling me I should at least see him, and who knows what might happen. Maybe we'd even get back together again'.

For fifteen minutes Joan raged, and no intervention was needed. From time to time she appealed to me to agree that it was awful, or that they were all unforgivable, but these were only rhetorical questions, needing no reply. After a time, however, the tone of her anger changed, and it became more helpless, so that instead of an avenging spirit she sounded like a defeated and trapped tigress. And as the hopelessness sounded in her voice, so the energy diminished and her whole body slumped. When she fell silent, I said after a short silence, 'You appear to feel the anger is no use, that "they" will win in the end?'

'They always have. I don't really count or I'm not strong enough and they can't or won't hear me.'

'And because "they" can't/won't hear or see you, you feel no one will?'

After considering this, Joan said:

'Well, I know that's not really true, because Seán hears me, and my granny used to hear me.'

Joan spoke of her granny, whom she loved dearly, and with whom she lived during school holidays. With her, Joan felt special and 'real'. She died when Joan was fifteen years of age.

'So some people can hear you, and you feel some cannot?'

Joan accepted this, and went on to discuss whether the difference was in her or in the other people. Did she approach people differently, did she voice her message less clearly to some people?

'Do you know, when I'm afraid of someone, I think in advance that what I am going to say will make them angry, and I only half say it. I used to feel so good when Declan and I met first, he seemed to really like me, and that was great. But then bit by bit he drank more and more, and I'm terrified of drunk men. My dad was never there when I was small, and when he did appear, I remember him as loud and noisy. I was afraid of him, and when he finally disappeared, I was glad. But then I was afraid because my Mam used to sink into silence and you couldn't talk to her.'

Again Joan looked back to a childhood of silence and fear, lightened by snatches of happiness which showed her that life could be different. After a long pause, she said:

'I was frightened a lot of the time, and I'm not going to have it like that for Seán. I suppose I'm afraid Seán will be frightened by Declan, and I'm trying to weigh up which would be best for Seán: to see a father who might frighten him, or not to see a father at all. Can you tell me which would be worse?'

This was a very direct question, at the end of a session. The temptation was to respond with some words of wisdom, although I believe it would not be possible in any discipline to give a certain answer. Even to spend more time looking at the *possible* outcomes with Joan would have been no more than guesswork, and as Joan would still be making the decision on her own in the end, I felt it was important to respect Joan's knowledge of her son, of Declan, of the circumstances, and also to respect her decision to explore these in the counselling meetings, in order to make a clearer choice. I replied:

'I honestly don't know, but I can hear how hard it is for you to make this choice. Perhaps we can examine the options and look closer at the possibilities next week'.

I found it hard to end this session, leaving Joan in the middle of trying to decide such an important step in her life. However, I felt I had indicated to her that she was not entirely alone, and that I had heard and understood her difficulty. Although I was not prepared (or able) to lift the burden of responsibility from her, I was willing to be with her in her choices and decisions.

## Session 5

I started this session aware that Joan had agreed to come for six sessions, so this might be our second last. As I had suggested at the end of Session 4 that we might look at her choices, I felt it was important that Joan be aware that I was not only listening but retaining the information she gave me, so I opened the session by saying:

'We ended last week talking about the difficulties around choosing whether or not to allow Declan to see Seán. But I'm aware too that this decision will have a great impact on you'.

This was a reminder about where we had ended, but it also focused on Joan herself, lest she concentrate solely on the impact on Seán, or whether or not to punish Declan for his previous abandonment.

'I've been thinking a lot about this, and I can see that I need to be happy myself with my decision, and not just choose for Seán, because if I hate it, then I'll be cross and angry around him. And I think that's what I'd like to look at – the effect of my choice on *me*. If Declan was dead, then Seán would have to survive without a father.'

This brought Joan's attention back on herself and her responsibility around her choice, rather than focusing on Seán and Declan, neither of whom were here or were in a position to make that decision.

'And I think I'd be OK if he were to see him perhaps once a month, with me, to begin with. I can't imagine it somehow, but I suppose it will just happen.'

I reminded her, 'You were quite sure you didn't want Declan in your flat, that that was your place.'

'Yes, but Mam's would be worse.'

Joan was beginning to sound panicky, as if the whole idea was starting to be too much even to think about. I realised that she'd been thinking about the idea, but had no notion of how to go about this.

'Perhaps a public place like McDonalds or the Zoo would be easier to begin with?'

Joan seized on the idea of a public place, and looked at several options open to her, and decided also to put a time limit of perhaps an hour or so on the meeting. However, the panic and fear which had threatened her previously returned when she began to consider the idea of meeting Declan again.

'The truth of it is I don't want to meet him at all. He tells me what to do and I get mad – and then I do it anyway. So getting mad is no good, I just end up raging, the way I used to with my brother. Raging inside but outside having to give in. Having to give in and become a skivvy like with my dad. Always the same story. Men win out every time.'

Joan here has connected the three principal male figures in her life: father, brother and boyfriend. Her reactions to each of them appears to be quite similar. Fear and powerlessness, followed by inner rage which has no outlet. Her childhood experiences still colour her current feelings and reactions, so that she cannot see clearly that she is her own adult person today, independent of all three, and if she wishes, independent of men altogether. Just now she is caught up in her anger, but cannot deal with or operate within it, until she sees the fear underlying it.

'I'm aware that you're very angry with them all, but I sense also that you feel helpless, and afraid of that helplessness.'

There was a long silence, and I wondered if I'd been correct, or if Joan was too angry and therefore too far from the fear to acknowledge it. Then she almost whispered:

'Yes, helpless. When Declan walked away, and when my dad disappeared, I had no one to be angry at. They just weren't there. They were gone. I was alone, the way Mam and I were alone.'

And Joan wept for the ache of loneliness and the fear of being abandoned and rejected.

The session ended shortly after, and before she left, I reminded her that next week was our sixth session and we could look then at whether or not she wanted to continue.

## Session 6

When Joan came for Session 6, I sensed some reserve in her, something guarded, as if she were about to tell me some bad or uncomfortable news. I tried to put this idea to one side because it could also distract me from paying full attention to where she was in her own story. She began by saying firmly:

'I'm going to meet Declan with Seán next week. We're going to meet in the Zoo. Seán will have something to distract him a little and it's as public as you can get. I'll see what Declan wants and we can take it from there.'

I said, 'You've taken the decision to contact him, and I sense you're pleased to have that resolved.'

Joan looked a bit surprised, as if she'd expected me to protest, to warn caution, to say 'are you sure?', 'is this wise?'

'Perhaps you expected me to advise you to do something else, or not to move too quickly?'

Joan laughed and admitted that she was surprised that I would accept any decision of hers without criticism. Her initial reserve had been defensive, ready to be challenged and hoping she could justify her decision. My willingness to accept that she was the best judge of her own situation and wishes was new to her, and she was pleased to be trusted. She spoke at length about her possible future, and that of Seán:

'I'm tired of being on my own. It's very hard to manage. Mam says she heard Declan may be back for good, so I could share the responsibility with him when Seán is sick and so on. Don't get me wrong – I wouldn't be without him. In fact I'd love a whole clatter of kids. But they're hard work on your own.'

This was becoming a businesslike session, with Joan extending her story into the future. I was aware that she was also drawing a veil over much of what she had experienced in the last session.

'I think I'll make this our last session, and I know I've looked at a lot of stuff I never really realised before, but that'll have to wait for another time. I think that once I know that I *can* manage on my own, even though I don't like it, then I'm not as afraid. I can tell them all to stuff it any time I like. And I can also go to counselling again, and rev up my batteries.'

Joan's smile as she said this softened the impact on me, but it had suddenly sounded as if she viewed counselling as a tonic one took when one was mentally run-down, and almost portrayed our work as quick-fire and mechanical. I had to remind myself that people look on counselling with different eyes and often with very different agendas. There was also a note of pleading in there somewhere, which I almost missed in my focus on myself.

'If you want to come back at any time, of course you may contact me again.'

Not all counsellors believe that such promise of future availability is wise, but I think that it creates a link with available resources, and as such, is beneficial. Most clients do not avail of the offer, and for those who do, it can happen that I will not be available, or have moved to another agency.

'It's good to know that I can. Maybe when the dust settles.'

I felt it would be helpful to highlight the important areas we had looked at, and which she decided not to pursue, rather than allow them to hang there, unmentioned or ignored.

'We did identify your underlying fear which fuels your anger, old and present, and I'm aware that you've chosen to leave this aside for the moment. Perhaps having become aware of it means that it will be more possible to explore it at another time, and it may give you a better understanding of what's happening for you in the meantime.'

Joan said goodbye and thanked me for my help and wished me well. There was a sense of escape, as if she'd expected me to try to persuade her not to leave, or try to push her again into expression of painful feelings. I was glad to see her new-found confidence around decisions and plans, but somewhat deflated also. I could imagine that confidence readily vanishing if faced by powerful men in her life, or by her mother instilling dependence. I found myself also uneasy about her spoken wish for more children, and the possibility of Declan being back in the country for good. I feared for her returning to live with a potentially violent man, who could bully and terrify her as he did before.

But of course this unease and this fear are *my* feelings, and it is important not only that I acknowledge them, but that I also allow them, experience them, and move beyond them. Unfinished business is a hazard of counselling, because clients invite us briefly into their lives, and equally need to send us on our way when their work is done. And we need to go, without leaving behind us a legacy or residue of guilt: 'I helped you and therefore you should not leave me totally!'

On the positive side, I believe Joan derived many benefits from her six sessions. She moved very quickly to trusting me and the work, this willingness fuelled by her need to protect and care for little Seán, but also perhaps hampered by her lack of independence and mobility in caring for him. Her connection with her fears around the men in her life, and her discovery of how this fear had been masked by anger and rage, usually futile, gave her an insight into her own self that she will not easily lose or ignore in the future. Her acknowledgement that she can manage well on her own if necessary, and her new confidence in her own judgement and ability, may well be sufficient to enable her to resist being a victim, powerless in the face of aggression or desertion.

I was glad to have worked with Joan, and sorry to see her go so soon. Would she have stayed longer and done more work if I had been different, kinder, sterner, given more direct advice? Maybe. And would that have been to her benefit? Who knows.

I never heard from her again.

#### REFERENCES

1. Kirschenbaum, H. and Henderson, V. Land (eds), *The Carl Rogers Reader* (London: Constable, 1990), p. 127-8.

# CHAPTER 5

*The only reality I can possibly know is the world as I perceive and experience it at this moment. The only reality you can possibly know is the world as you perceive and experience it at this moment. And the only certainty is that those perceived realities are different.*[1]

## CLIENT TWO: JOE

Joe's employer suggested that he see a counsellor, because of difficulties with colleagues at work. He therefore came reluctantly and resentfully, merely 'because the boss said'. When he rang me to make the appointment, he spoke very loudly on the phone, and sounded angry, complaining at the appointment times I offered him, hoping I'd be on time as he was a very busy man, and expressing horror at my fee. He sounded so reluctant that I was surprised when he finally appeared.

I illustrate here six pivotal sessions of his twenty-two. Our work progressed very slowly to begin with, and our relationship struggled to survive. Perhaps it would be true to say also that I struggled to survive within it, as Joe was a forceful and powerful person.

### Session 1
Joe arrived fifteen minutes early, and was quite annoyed that I asked him to wait until our appointed time.

'I have to get back to work, I've left an important meeting to be here' and 'the least you could do is see me now that I'm here'.

I believe it is important to hold the boundaries of time as exactly as I can, because this, over time, reassures the client that

I keep my word (an hour means an hour and a set time means that time), that I am consistent (this applies for every session), that the stated hour will not be prolonged, and that there is safety for the client in that set time. For example, clients often mention something five minutes before a session is over, knowing that there will not be time to consider or discuss it until the next session, and not wanting it talked of today. If the hour were to be extended, arbitrarily by me, then the subject would be faced immediately, before they were ready. (When I first started counselling work, I saw a client who travelled quite a long distance. I often 'allowed' her to continue past the hour because I felt she 'needed' this. One day when we were fifteen minutes over time, she asked please could she go now, as she had to collect a child from school. Since then, I have been much more careful about boundaries!)

Joe started by telling me, loudly, that he was thirty-eight, married, no children, working in a bank, not promoted as he felt he deserved.

'And now I'm sent to a counsellor, a shrink. Let me tell you first off that I don't think you'll be able to do anything for me. I'm here under orders. And I'm wide awake. No brainwashing me.'

Joe was a big man, and he seemed to fill the small room we were in. He was very angry and barely civil, and physically quite frightening. Part of me wanted to placate him, to reassure him that I wasn't a threat to him. He needed to assert himself, to cover up the needy part of himself, the self that had been ordered like a small child to look for help. I sensed that he would hear very little of anything I said right now.

'You don't really want to be here at all?'

'I sure as hell don't. What can you do? Helping professions! I read the papers and I know the jargon. Not much help around. I went to my doctor last month about my headaches, and he said "psychosomatic". So now I'm psycho. You're all the same, if you'll excuse the expression, bloody parasites. Making money out of misery. And big money too.'

I found it difficult to withstand this barrage of anger without responding, but I was also aware that wherever the anger was directed, it was not against me personally. Joe didn't know *me*, and he was inveighing against a system, 'fixers' as he saw them, and anything and anybody who got in his way just now.

'Are you just going to sit there and say nothing? Surely you have to *do* something to earn the money?'

'I hear you saying how awful the system is, and how much you hate being instructed to come here.'

It would have been easy to produce words of some kind of wisdom in response to Joe's pressure, or to speak some defence of 'helpers'. There was also a temptation to defend my profession against the 'making money out of misery' accusation, and to produce some kind of 'diagnosis' or 'homework exercise' as a tangible product for Joe to take away in return for his money. Instead I tried to sit with the expression of rage, because this is Joe as he is right now. He continued to give out about politicians, tax, colleagues, asking rhetorical questions and allowing no space for response. I felt that not only was he venting his rage, but that he was also fending off anything I might want to say, holding me at arm's length, and blocking any input on my part. He was demanding action from me, but at the same time he was determined that he wouldn't give me any space to do or say anything. His need to dominate the session was very great.

Finally I got a space to say:

'Our time is almost up, and if you feel you want to come back, perhaps we could agree to meet for six sessions initially. After that we can look further down the road. This is the way the sessions would be, exploring together your concerns. I would like also to say that our work will be totally confidential. I will not be reporting back to your employer, nor to your doctor.'

Joe appeared to be quite taken aback that an hour had passed, but also showed no desire to linger. He escaped out of the room like someone released from a trap. I felt that it had been important to underline the confidential nature of our work, since he had come at the bidding of his employer. I would probably have to repeat this at a later stage, when he is more open to really hearing what I say. I was aware that I was exhausted by the session, and realised that I had been braced throughout as if ready to defend myself against attack. I need to examine this reaction on my part, because if this were to continue, then my congruence or genuineness would be lessened, and instead of sitting openly with Joe, I would be sitting concentrated on my own self, with only half of me free to be with Joe.

The key words or statements I heard during the hour, and which I want to hold in my mind for future reference, are his apparent fear of being changed or altered or controlled by someone else ('brainwashing', 'fixers'), resentment about not being promoted ('as he deserved'), fear of anyone seeing his private world (his determination that I would not get a word said, his holding me outside). I also had a question about his loudness. Is he partially deaf, is he trying to control others by shouting them down, is he afraid no one will listen to him if he speaks softly, or is it some other reason altogether that I have no inkling of as yet? I hope he will continue to come as there is an overall sensation of a very unhappy person, seeking desperately for change.

## Session 4

By the time Session 4 came around, there was little apparent change in Joe's approach. Session 2 and 3 had proceeded in the same vein as the first, and Joe still presented as overbearing, loud and unapproachable. The whole world was against him, everyone was out to do him down, and I was beginning to wilt.

Somehow Joe was challenging me to be the person he wanted me to be, who would fight back and disagree. By not engaging in a way familiar to him, by remaining silent, I was 'winning'.

'I can't stand the way you won't give advice or ask questions. You just sit and look at me. I know you must be mad at me. And how can I tell you more if you won't ask questions?'

'You're used to people getting angry and hassling you, and in some way, in order to go on, you need me to push you and lean on you?'

'Yes! You put it to me and I can defend myself.'

The important thing here seemed not to engage in the tussle the client was intent on provoking. His use of the image of defending himself was illuminating, with its expectation of being attacked, and perhaps of feeling in some way being tested, or being insecure in the relationship. I was trying to understand where Joe was at, in all his rage and frustration, while remaining accepting of him. In this way I hoped to use the relationship between us, without ignoring and concealing any aspect of it, and without engaging or fuelling his current feelings. If I were to try to 'mask' or 'cure' this anger, because it was uncomfortable or threatening for me, then I would have been denying an aspect of Joe that was very real. By communicating my experience of him as an angry person just now, but accepting this as his current *feeling* rather than as his total person, I hoped to facilitate Joe's own awareness of his anger, and a belief that it's all right to be angry.

If change is the desired goal of counselling (no one who is fully happy and content with the way they are comes to counselling!), the only way real change can be brought about is through a deeper awareness of ourselves and the kind of people we are: 'What am I really feeling, underneath these façades and behind these defences?' 'Is this how I want to be, how I want to relate to others?' Counselling provides a reflective space with an accepting listener, within which the client feels safe enough to dismantle his old, and no longer effective, defences.

'The wife is pushing me. She says I should ask for a raise in the new discussions. She mustn't be listening to me at all. I've told her over and over again that no one at work gives a damn about me or my worries.'

Joe moved abruptly from looking at our relationship, and while I was aware of the distancing implicit in the phrase 'the *wife*', this was the first time Joe had moved from the job to his wife and home. I thought it possible that he might be feeling that no one anywhere is listening to him, and this might include me as a counsellor. This oblique reference to his wife may be as close as he can safely come to accusing me of not listening.

'Perhaps you feel I'm not listening to you right here, right now?'

By highlighting this possibility, I moved back into the immediacy of our relationship in this session. I hoped it would open a new path of exploration between us, a willingness perhaps to discuss the feelings of being ignored, which seemed to be an underlying theme in Joe's story to date. However, I was not particularly surprised when Joe shot back:

'Of course you are. That's your job, isn't it?'

We sat in silence while the sharp answer echoed around the room. And then Joe said, in an unusually quiet voice:

'Actually I do feel you are listening. And that's quite different. I expect you'd allow me to go on and on. But I'm afraid too: of what you'll make of what I say; that you'll see beyond my words. I'm afraid of what you'll see inside me.'

'You're afraid I'll see inside you and that I won't like what I see?'

'Well you couldn't like it. Nobody could. And who cares anyway?'

'I sense you're pushing me away again, and that you'd almost prefer I'd get angry back at you, rather than listen to you.'

'You're trying to get inside me, and then you'll tell me how awful I am. Not fit to live, and no good for anything.'

'That's happened to you before?'

'Of course it has. For years. My mother used to store up everything I did and tell my father when he came home. Always late. And then he'd wake me up and leather me. So I'd never tell her anything, and I still don't. She still tells him I'm no good. She's impossible. I could kill her sometimes.'

'You sound really angry with her?'

'No – I don't. She's marvellous for her age. Everyone says so.'

'Well – perhaps you don't see eye-to-eye all the time.'

'I don't see her very often. It's hard to get away.'

'And when you do see her?'

'My father and herself are living in a different world. You have to remember that.'

Having picked up on Joe's annoyance and underlying anger towards his mother, I found Joe was unwilling to look closely at this. Determined to protect himself from acknowledging threatening feelings, Joe used what may be a learned conversational technique of side-stepping and obscuring the topic, and shifting the focus on to his mother's age, his own busy life, the unreality of his parents' world. I tried once again:

'You find it hard to acknowledge that you're angry with her. If my mother did that, I'd be raging.'

This was an effort to bring Joe's reluctance out into the open, and lest this reluctance was caused by fear that his anger would not be acceptable to me, in effect gave him 'permission' by saying how it would be for me.

But Joe was not ready to acknowledge his anger towards her, and I did not want to continue to 'push' him to a point where he was not ready to go. Instead I stored what he had said and what he seemed to feel, knowing that such a stoutly defended emotion was likely to arise again, and he might then be more able and willing to explore it, and to acknowledge it.

'She used to tell me how bad I was, and how I'd go to hell, and the devils would get me. And at school they had more of it. Rubbish of course. But it stays with you. I read somewhere that in India they beat drums and clash cymbals to chase away bad spirits. That's what I need to do.'

Joe laughed. I realised this was the first time I'd seen any sign of humour or lightness in him. And already he was distancing himself from what he had shared.

'Surely our time is up.'

And I also realised that he had not been shouting for the last ten minutes, when his voice rose again blusteringly:

'I don't know what you must think. Daft child, daft mother. A long time ago.'

I responded: 'It sounds very terrifying for a small boy. Perhaps we can look at it again next week'.

Joe left quite abruptly, paying his money without the usual remark about it being easily earned by some. My picture of him had deepened, and I was beginning to see beyond the forceful exterior to his inner person, frightened and full of self-loathing, trying to maintain his energetic and false mask of containment and power. I hoped to return to his lack of self-worth, his guilt about being bad, and the images of devils, which remain so vividly with him.

## Session 9

My sense of Joe had changed by Session 9. Where a client has erected a wall to protect his inner self from perceived criticism or ridicule, then the counsellor needs to decide how to proceed. A head-on attempt to break down such a barrier can result merely in the client retreating behind a further inner defence. I feel it is vital that the client himself take down this defence, piece by piece, risking the exposure of his real self. The role of the counsellor is to express and accept the existence of the defence, to acknowledge the client's need for such a rampart between himself and the world, and his extreme reluctance either to take it down, or emerge from behind it. Such acknowledgement will, in the words of one of my students, 'melt the cement' in the wall, render it less necessary, and encourage attempts to step beyond it.

During Sessions 5-8, Joe spent a lot of time painfully telling me about his childhood, his violent father (who beat him methodically, without visible anger), his fear and his urgent need to be the achieving person his parents desired. During Session 9 he casually said:

'And during the bank raid, I was so afraid they'd just shoot me and that would be that. I could have done something, anything, like you see on TV. Reached for the alarm, stood up to them, but no. I was just frozen to the chair. I tell you, I'd have done anything they asked. My father was right – no gumption. I never stood up to him either.'

All the bluster was gone, and Joe was looking at the self he didn't like, the self who was fearful and timid, reminiscent of the small boy afraid of his father's late-night home-comings, afraid of devils. I was reminded of a previous client who saw himself as a 'snowflake', immensely fragile and insecure, here this second and disappeared into nothingness the next, without impact or trace left behind. And I was tempted to respond with encouragement, with reassurance that anyone would be afraid in those circumstances, that 'snowflakes can be built into snowmen'. Instead I acknowledged the fear of that incident, and indeed the fear in him right now, with the beads of sweat visible on his forehead.

'It's frightening even to remember it. Would you like to tell me more about it?'

And he did. It had taken nine sessions for Joe to share this pivotal event in his life, this defining moment which had linked in with the small terrified boy he had hidden for so long beneath a loud and angry exterior, and the importance of which he appeared to have denied even to himself. He told me unemotionally of the masked men appearing suddenly, holding a gun to his head while everyone else had to lie on the floor, being able to smell the terror of the robbers and the way the guns shook in their hands as he waited for violence and death. And while his voice remained unemotional, his whole body shook and trembled.

I reminded myself that my task was not merely to watch my client in distress, but to be with him, while never forgetting that it is Joe's distress, not mine. The willingness of the counsellor to stay within the fear of the client, without attempting to rescue or comfort, without allowing my own feelings to add to his burden, is difficult but essential. And I became aware that to be alone in such distress is perhaps the loneliest place one can be, and I was glad that I was there with Joe, and glad that he could re-experience, or at least describe, these terrible events.

And he finished with:

'Look at me. It's five years ago and I'm shaking.'

The self-loathing in his voice was plain to hear.

'And I know what you're thinking. That I'm a coward and a useless person to have around.'

And he wouldn't meet my eye, so certain was he that I'd despise him.

I said: 'It was a horrific experience. I've never faced anything like that. I sense that while it's still frightening to think about, you're also hating yourself because you didn't do something else at the time?'

I thought it important to acknowledge the impact of such an event, to acknowledge also his fear, and try to look beyond to his self-loathing, which appears to be blocking his recognition and acceptance of his fear, and his ability to move forward through and with that fear.

I didn't spend time assuring him that I wasn't thinking badly of him, because that would be merely using words which would not convince him. I felt it would be better to continue on in my tacit acceptance of him as he was there and then, so that eventually, hearing neither criticism nor judgement, he could become aware that I was able to accept all aspects of him. The hope, of course, is that, in becoming aware of my acceptance over time, he will become able to accept himself as he is.

Joe spent the remainder of this session telling me of different episodes in his life which showed him to be disappointing to himself. He saw himself as a failure in all aspects, and he linked this to his father's stated expectations and reproaches, which were engraved on his memory. 'I never thought a son of mine would…', 'You'll never amount to much', and 'How could you let us down?' were part of a long litany of impossible standards and grinding criticisms which Joe had now taken as his own, and applied even more rigorously to himself every day. Having adopted his 'locus of evaluation' from his apparently over-critical father, he failed every day to reach these imagined standards. And to fail every day is corrosive to one's self-esteem. I think Joe was glad to leave this session also!

## Session 10

Joe came to this session almost eagerly, and launched at once into an expansion of how he was failing to live up to other people's expectations. He remembered his mother's favourite phrase, 'Make your father proud of you', and his awareness that when he 'failed' to do something, he was letting both his parents down, and hurting or wounding those whom he loved. So somehow the beatings his father administered were 'for his own good' to help him become tougher and more able to become the child they wanted.

A connection occurred to me which seemed important enough to share.

'Perhaps the bank and your superiors have taken the place of your father or both your parents, and you feel they cannot be proud of you after the raid?'

The ensuing silence was so long, I feared that this connection might have been made too soon, before he was ready to hear it or consider whether it was valid or not.

'You know, it's funny you say that. I do have the distinct feeling that I let them down, that they deserved something more from me. During our training it was always onwards and upwards, nothing was ever good, it was only a step towards a greater effort. And always an agenda of possible reward if we tried harder, but we never seemed to arrive. The standards were high and became higher every year. The goalposts constantly changed and it was like chasing a pot of gold. But the other message was how good the bank was to us, with cheap loans, good pensions, status – and what were we prepared to do in return? And it does sound like when I was small, always on about how good they were to me and all they did for me and sacrificed for me, and what did I do in return? I let them down.'

'Are you saying that you feel that the bank is punishing you by not promoting you, because you've let them down?'

I suggested the connection between the lack of promotion and his father's beatings, because he had not appeared angry at not being promoted, nor at being beaten, but rather felt a resigned, deep-seated resentment that these follow on from his 'failure' to live up to others' expectations.

'That's rubbish. They're just mean and cruel. Holding out carrots that you cannot reach. I wouldn't take their old promotions if they begged me.'

Joe suddenly sounded like a boy who has been refused sweets, saying who wants your old sweets anyway!

'And I wouldn't promote myself. When I'm asked to do anything different, I make a point of saying no. I'm afraid of being pushed around. I can stand up for myself, and I'll do only as much as it takes to get the job done. I'm not going to give in to these bullies.'

Joe's voice had risen, and he was glaring at me as if I was a boss demanding that he do something against his will.

'I can hear you are much louder and angry at even the thought of someone "pushing you around", "out to get you", as if they had expectations and you weren't able to meet them. I'm wondering what your expectations are of yourself?'

This was a challenging statement, an effort to help Joe to look at himself, rather than at himself *in relation* to others. He took it on board quite readily, and in effect, turned to look at himself.

It seemed important to help Joe differentiate between his own aims and dreams, and what he believed were those of others in his life. In effect, to recognise that his locus of evaluation was firmly outside of himself, and that he appeared to measure his own worth in terms of meeting the standards of other people.

He needed to live his own life, not a life contorted into a different shape in an attempt to please others. If Joe could move away from trying to second-guess others, then he might be able to see how he was living, and perhaps move to make choices, and set his own standards.

'Well, to have a nice home and a good job, and maybe a family one day. Is that what you mean?'

'So you're saying you have achieved at least some of these aims, but somehow this isn't quite enough? That others appear to be saying you must do more, you must satisfy their expectations? How would you like the next ten years to be?'

'I wish I could just stop waiting to be punished, as if God had a big stick to beat me with. And as I say that I can see my own father.'

There was a reflective silence.

'I'd like to think about that and come back to it at the next session. All this is very new to me.'

I was aware that this session had been quite heady, but also that Joe for most of the time had laid aside his blustering and defensive self, and had been really present in the session, as his fundamental basic self, his organismic self.

## Session 16

For the next five sessions, Joe looked at his own aims and dreams, which up to now had been obscured by his focus on others, by his need to repay others, and by his fear of looking too closely at ambitions because in doing so, he might aim at them and fail. Failure, as he saw it, to meet the demands of others, real or imagined, had attuned him to the idea of himself as a 'failure'. The effort to acknowledge that he could choose his own objectives, and succeed at them, was both new and difficult to accept. He had mentioned his image of God as being a punitive one, and he spent some time linking this with his authoritarian father, whom he appeared to have both loved and hated in equal measure. But he had spoken mostly about his relationship with his wife, to whom he had been married for five years. She was some years younger than he, and although they had both spoken generally about wanting children, this hadn't happened for them. Although he had mentioned his own disappointment at this, he had also said it was hard to talk to his wife about this whole matter because he felt any discussion was a reflection on him, and an accusation about yet another failure on his part.

So although the relationship appeared to be good and loving, there were no-go areas where he wouldn't venture, and to which he denied her access. I felt this needed to be addressed, as he appeared to be circling it, and perhaps he was asking tacitly for help in facing it head on.

'I'm aware that it is difficult for you to speak with Ann about your feelings on certain topics, like trying for a family, and perhaps about the sexual side of your relationship. And I'm wondering if you are perhaps afraid she'll think less of you, or disapprove of you?'

I had an idea that, while he had been able to become more assertive and self-confident at work, his need for approval was still an obstacle in his personal relationships, based on a wish not to 'let other people down, after all they'd done for him'.

'I know she must despise me, because she's been to doctors and all, and I just can't bear to go. So it's obviously my fault that we can't have kids.'

'You know she despises you?'

'Well, she obviously hasn't said so. But she must. And anyway, I don't want to talk about it.'

And his voice rose in the old familiar way, as he let me know in no uncertain terms that I was trespassing on unsafe territory, but this time I didn't back away.

'It's hard for you to talk about it. And I sense you don't allow

Ann to see your real feelings about this, just as you're closing me out now. Perhaps she thinks you don't really want children?'

'She must know. I've always wanted a family.'

'I'm not sure. Have you told her in so many words? If you get angry when it comes up, she may be getting a different message – that perhaps you're not interested in children?'

There was a long silence. I sensed Joe was tracking back to see if he could remember a time when he and Ann had actually, and honestly, discussed his wishes to have a family, and his fear of disappointing her and 'letting her down'.

'I suppose I assume she must know. And honestly I'm afraid to have a medical check. If they say I can't have children, then it's real. It's out and it's known. And then what will we do.'

There was a note of despair in Joe's voice.

'So as long as it's not said clearly, then there's hope it may not be so. But once it's said, it can never be changed?'

I didn't fully understand the reason for the despair, but it was real and struck a cold note of inevitability and of impending disaster.

'Obviously not. But if I can keep them from saying it, then they might change their minds. Otherwise there's no going back.'

'I sense we're talking more than doctors here?'
And Joe told me about his sense, as a child, that if he could

deflect the naming of a situation, then it mightn't happen, and every day without it being mentioned was a day gained. Specifically he spoke of his fear of his parents separating, because he had heard them say in relation to their neighbours' many problems: 'We always knew they were having trouble, but it's out in the open now, and there's no going back'. And the neighbours were duly separated, or convicted, or in trouble of one sort or another. And that phrase – 'it's out in the open now, and there's no going back' – had been his mantra. His childhood aim, continued unconsciously and automatically into adulthood, was to keep difficult and painful experiences hidden, and never to speak of them, lest 'there be no going back'.

'So when people come close to saying what you don't want to happen, you try to head them off, perhaps by changing the subject or by talking them down?'

'It sounds as if I bully them a bit? But I don't mean to. I'm just afraid they'll say it.'

'And when you're afraid, you get angry and keep people out.'

'I know. But I don't know how to change.'

'Well, I'm aware you've named and said out how you react, and where that comes from. And that wasn't easy to look at. Are you saying you'd like to react differently, perhaps to allow yourself and others to name more of where they're at and what they'd like? And that maybe by talking about it, it can be changed, and that possibly there is "going back"?'

'Something like that. But it's very big.'
This session appeared to have afforded great insight for Joe.

He had acknowledged his long-term need to cover and hide important topics, and his angry fear lest others break that taboo, and his resulting bullying in order to control them. He had also expressed his desire to be different and to act differently, to face down his private demons, and while acknowledging that this would be difficult, he had not despaired of his ability to so change.

At the end of Session 19, as a 'doorknob' remark, Joe had mentioned the possibility of ending our work, and of shortly going away on holidays. In order to assure him that I had heard what he had said as he went out the door, I brought this up at the start of the next session. He appeared to be quite hesitant, half-saying he'd like to end, half-mentioning the holiday, and then saying of course it was what *I*, as the 'expert', recommended that was important. I acknowledged his embarrassment, and asked if endings were difficult for him, and he said:

'Oh yes! Usually I just walk away, don't appear again. It's easier than facing someone's disappointment or persuasion to continue. I remember when I left home for the first time I was nineteen. I just got on the boat. I rang them later to say I was alive, and even doing that was hard.'

'So making the decision to end here, and taking the courage to speak about it, is new for you?'

'Oh yes! You're privileged!'

And Joe laughed, and then went on:

'So much of what I'm doing is new, I didn't want just to walk away this time.'

'I sense you've quite a lot to look at, and much of it is new?'

And Joe told proudly of making an appointment with his doctor concerning his wish to have a child, about speaking to his immediate boss about his fear of being in the public office in the bank, and if that were in the way of his promotion, perhaps they could look at other avenues of advancement, and of having a good discussion with his wife about his fears and longings in relation to having a baby. This was a different person before me, reviewing for himself as much as for me, the changes he had made. And above all, he conveyed the sense of freedom and empowerment it gave him to have taken these steps.

'So I'm taking a month off and we'll go away to the sun. I plan to go in three weeks' time, and I thought that I might make that a break from here too! Then if needs be, maybe I could come back in the autumn?'

'You don't want to shut the door fully, just in case…?'

'Well, it seems such a final step. And maybe I'm not ready to leave. Maybe it's a mistake.'

'Perhaps we could arrange to meet twice more, to look at endings for you, and how it is difficult to take responsibility for what may appear like a final step?'

'That sounds good. And I'll have time for two sessions before I go on holidays.'

And that's what we did. During those last two sessions, we looked at the pain of closing a door, and how endings do not have to be rejections. This was especially important, because for Joe, ending relationships had always had a kind of violence attached, a throwing away rather than a letting go. We each acknowledged how we would be sad to see the sessions end, but that the sadness was normal, expected, and while painful, was also a tribute to the importance of our work together.

And we also reviewed that work, and the decisions and actions Joe had been able to make once he acknowledged and accepted the hidden and dark places in himself. And importantly, we acknowledged that the work was not over for Joe, that he would still find self-sharing difficult, and that risking his inner self to the glare of potential criticism might always demand an effort. We looked also at how easily the ability to be one's own evaluer can be swept away in response to a single word or look from someone important to us, or someone with authority over us. I underlined how much more difficult it is to *unlearn* something and then learn something new, than it is to learn something from scratch. Joe reminded himself that one of the greatest changes for him had been the realisation that if he wanted his message, his opinion, to be heard by someone else, he had to deliver it clearly, without anger, without bluster, without being defensive, without shouting. His fear of not being heard had often been the main cause of no one listening because, not being able to claim attention from others as his right, he fudged and diluted the message he was trying to convey. Assuming responsibility for his part in communication was quite new.

Overall, these were two good sessions, clarifying and consolidating Joe's progress. I was sorry to see him go, but glad that he felt able to go. I did not see him again, but from time to time heard of him inadvertently, and he appeared to have maintained his progress, and this was good to hear.

#### REFERENCES

1.  Kirschenbaum, H. and Henderson, V. Land (eds), *The Carl Rogers Reader* (London: Constable, 1990), p. 424.

# CHAPTER 6

*...the relationship is one which provides the client with the opportunity of making responsible choices, in an atmosphere in which it is assumed that he is capable of making decisions for himself*[1]

## CLIENT THREE: MAURA

Depression in a client can be very difficult to tolerate. We can feel helpless without pills or potions, and it is often difficult to go on believing that we have anything of value to offer in the face of hopelessness. The phrase that I use to reassure myself is 'Trust in the process', because theoretically I fully subscribe to the belief that listening to, accepting and staying with a client is in itself therapeutic. This client has brought herself to the point of seeking help, therefore she is not beyond help. Some part of her still believes that she can be helped.

I can offer myself as companion in a safe relationship, and the experience of being with another human being, who is neither critical nor impatient nor intolerant, will of itself effect change of some measure. 'I may feel hopeless, but I am not alone, therefore...' This is the process that I trust.

### Session 1

Maura came to see me one grey November day, slight and timid, aged forty-three, referred by an ex-client from three years before. She told me she was separated for the last nine years, with three grown-up children, aged nineteen, twenty-one and twenty-two, two girls and a boy. She had come looking for help because she had recently been suffering from panic attacks, and what she thought might be 'mild agoraphobia' and depression. Life appeared to be pointless, her last child had moved into a flat in town, she had little contact with her ex-husband, and she really didn't know why she was bothering to come for counselling. She spoke in a monotone and without energy, relating facts as if they concerned someone else.

'I work in a legal office, but I'm really just a glorified typist, a dog's body for everyone else. I used to have more friends but just lately I can't be bothered going out, and people stop ringing in the end if you say no to everything. My parents are still alive, but they're down the country, and I don't go down often. I've a couple of brothers and a sister in the west too, but they rarely come up to the city.'

The overall note was listless and depressed, and Maura sounded as if she had come to please her friend, and while listing what she saw as important facts I'd need to know in order to 'cure' her, she didn't seem particularly interested in being in the session, or in anything else for that matter.

'Do you just want me to go on talking? I'm sure you've seen lots of people like me, hopeless and depressed, so you'll know what I should do. I sometimes think I'm going mad.'

This kind of hopeless appeal can be very seductive. It is difficult to sit with despair and helplessness, and the temptation can be to produce instant, and useless, solutions. Our natural instinct to help, to assist, can result in: 'Do this or try that. Of course you'll improve – just hang in there'. In reality, I do not know, and I cannot know, how this person will be in a month's time. It is important that I sit with her in all her unhappiness, rather than try to solve her barely stated difficulties.

The wish to reassure and support is very strong, but it may well be myself I am rescuing. A client's implicit trust in my 'expertise' can link into areas of doubt or insecurity in myself, and I may feel the need to justify my way of working, to give full measure to this client who has travelled a distance: in effect 'to produce the goods!' Trying to second-guess what a client means is wasted time and effort, and more often than not is inaccurate. 'Am I going mad?' is rarely a request for a technical discussion of stages of insanity. It is much more likely to be a cry for help from someone who is losing their ability to cope with their everyday life, who is frightened because the old stabilities have been rocked, who is terrified of an unknown future. Maura continued:

'Sometimes I get so depressed that I cannot think straight. I'm afraid of being locked up and getting ECT – I had an aunt who suffered from her nerves and we were all afraid of her when we were small.'

I responded to the fear she expressed, which seemed right now to be the thread running underneath the depression and being thought 'mad'.

'I sense you're quite afraid of what may happen to you if you go on feeling so low.'

But she backed away from following up on this, perhaps offered too soon if she is truly afraid of being afraid.

'I've no right to be so miserable. I have a nice house, lovely children, I'm not short of money, and I don't care for any of it.'

And she wept silently, noiselessly, with her face covered and her body rocking silently. Just as quickly she stopped and apologised profusely for crying. I said:

'Sometimes crying can be a release.'

'I hate it. The only place I can cry easily is in bed, with the covers over my head, then no one can hear me.'

'That sounds familiar, as if it's always been like that?'

'Oh yes. You never cried at home when I was small. There was no point, and it got you into trouble. And then of course I couldn't let my children see me crying, and my husband couldn't stand it. That's the way it's been – there were lots of things he couldn't stand.'

And she told me about her marriage which hadn't been happy, and she didn't know how she would have survived without her children.

'Now the last of them has moved out, and the house is very quiet.'

The session continued, with Maura retailing her unhappy life and her hopelessness, and as our time ended, she asked could she come back.

'It's nice to be able to talk. No one else much listens. Is this the way it goes, with me just talking?'

I explained that this was the way I worked, that we would have an hour each time, and that perhaps we could agree to meet for six sessions to begin with, and then extend this if we both felt it was going well. I feel it is important to allow my client to be in charge of her own attendance, to make a conscious choice each time she comes, or else she may come under pressure and reluctantly, or not at all. Agreeing to six sessions to begin with allows her (and me) an initial testing time, neither too short at two sessions, by which time we'd hardly be in a position to know enough to choose to work together, or too open-ended, suggesting a commitment of years ahead, like the 'analysis' joked about in films.

## Session 27

For twenty-five more sessions, Maura came faithfully each week, and each week she told me about what had happened since we last met, how unhappy she was, and about the different people in her life. Even though she was still somewhat depressed, her life seemed to be busier, and at times the room seemed to be full of other people, thronging in and out of her story, shades of her life companions, her children, her workmates. While it is of course important for us all to share our story and our headlines, in the effort to make ourselves understood, Maura was not accustomed to being in the spotlight. Aware of her discomfort and unease, I tried continually to focus on her own self, without frightening or jolting her:

'I'm aware that I'm hearing a lot about the people who are important to you, but I'm not hearing a lot about yourself? ...If I had so much on my plate, I'd lose sight of *me*, and I have an idea that's what happening to you now? ...It appears that your life is very crowded at times, and I'm not sure if you are getting lost in the middle?'

I tried to rephrase what she said in a more personal way, to give permission to express whatever feeling was troubling her at that moment, and just as persistently Maura fended me off, agreed 'Yes, but...' or brought yet another protagonist into her story. I discussed our 'stuckness' with my supervisor, I reminded myself of the importance of staying with the 'process' of Rogers, and I felt quite useless much of the time. I even found it difficult to stay awake on occasion, as the room appeared to empty of energy and interest.

In Session 27, Maura was even slower and less engaged than usual. Into my flatness and lack of energy, Maura said suddenly and almost vehemently:

'I feel you're not really listening to me any more, that you're not really interested in what I am saying'. Maura was risking an accusation of disinterest on my part, and she was more present in the session than I'd seen her before. I decided to acknowledge her risk-taking by being more open myself:

'Maura, there has been very little energy in our sessions lately, as if we were circling around something and avoiding it at the same time. My sense also is that, while I don't know what it is, I think you do. And perhaps you're cross with me that I cannot see it, and I am trying to understand, but I need you to make it plain.'

After a very long silence, during which Maura started several sentences which faded into silence again, she said in a low and tiny voice:

'I've never told anyone else this. It was our secret, and he said if I told, I'd be sent away. But he abused me once a week for years, and I loved him and I hated him, and now I can't bear to think about him.'

I assumed that Maura was talking about her father, but I was also aware that she had not precisely named him. I waited:

'I didn't really know what it was about, but I knew it was wrong because he made such a point about a secret. And we'd play great games first, and then this. And it used to hurt, and I'd cry and he'd get angry, so I stopped letting him know how much I hated it. And of course I couldn't tell anyone. Do you think I'm dreadful?'

An old shame was there, seeking reassurance from me that I didn't despise her. I said:

'I'm aware how painful it is for you still, and how difficult it is for you to talk about it. I sense also that it has haunted you for all these years'.

'Haunted – yes. His name was Terry and he was only ten years older than me. He used to babysit for ages every Saturday when my parents went out, and he was my only uncle. I used to think they must know, but I've thought about it since and I don't suppose they did. Do you think they did?'

Maura was looking back at her stolen childhood, and the desolation in her voice, and in the story she was telling, was very painful to sit with. I reminded myself that the experience and the pain was hers, and that any expression of my difficulty in listening to it would diminish and distract from her reliving and allowing of her anguish. She continued with facts and dates, until the enormity of what she was telling struck her, and she wept for a long time. I was aware of how much I felt like saying consoling words, or putting my arms around her, but either might have been a form of rescuing her. Sometimes a client may appear to need, to want, or even ask for the comfort of a holding or a hugging, and some counsellors consider this a valid step in the process. However, I fear it can halt the feelings of unhappiness and abandonment *for now*, and by closing down the current experience, might make it extremely difficult to reach that point of exploration again. A comforting hug might become the expected outcome of tears. Aware that 'we have no right to deny others their pain', I felt it was best to sit with her and allow her space to experience what had been closed off for so long. There is also the possibility that stepping into the role of physical comforter could bring my feelings of rage and anger against the abuser too close and too involved with my client's feelings. In order to travel with Maura without stifling her hurt, I needed to put my own feelings to one side. I felt that to share my reactions could be an added burden at this time, and eventually her sobs tailed away.

'I was so relieved when the whole family went to America. I remember thinking I'd never see him again, and no one need ever, ever know. I was about eleven, so it went on for five or six years. I remember my First Communion was a particularly bad time, not being able to tell and feeling so guilty. I think I've felt guilty all my life.'

'You felt somehow it was all your fault?'

'Yes, I suppose I did. And that sounds so silly when I say it. I was only six when it started. But surely I could have stopped as I got older. And then I read in the papers about "victim impact reports" and I tell myself I was a victim. And I don't want to be one all my life. Should I go to the police and report him, after all these years? And that feels silly too. Anyhow it's a long time ago.'

Maura was preparing to leave, as our hour was ended, putting on a 'public' face and distancing herself from her feelings of misery and despair, but darting glances at me as if to gauge my reactions to her disclosures. It was important to convey to her my willingness to be with her in her distress, along with my awareness that I could not solve her problems nor think for her. I needed to be quite explicit in conveying this willingness by saying, '*We* can find ways to explore, to look at…'. Remaining thus detached is not in any way saying 'You're on your own', but it is rather a statement of being ready to stay with her and to accompany her wherever she goes.

I felt it was important that Maura take away with her some idea of my unchanged regard for her, and acknowledgement of her willingness to trust me.

'This has been a very difficult session for you, and I'm aware that you have risked sharing a very hidden part of yourself. I'm glad you could trust me, and we can come back to this again next week.'

## Session 28

Maura came back for the next session, appearing relieved that she had broken the barrier of silence. She told me that her uncle had come back to her home place suddenly two years ago, and that he was known to be ill and everyone was so sorry for him and admiring of his courage in fighting his cancer.

'I find it impossible when everyone is praising him, and want to shout out what he did to me, but of course I can't, not even to my parents. So I just don't visit. And it has stirred up all the old feelings, and sometimes I hope he'll die soon, and then I feel awful.'

'You really feel you'd like to see him dead?'

If Maura were to say this to someone outside counselling, then the response she would probably get would be 'You mustn't say that', 'What a dreadful thing to wish on anyone', 'How could you, and he so sick?' In counselling it is important to focus on the expressed feeling and acknowledge and explore it, so that the client can own the feeling, accept herself within it, and plan her action from this new point. Telling herself she is a bad person, berating herself for feeling thus, only results in the feeling being kept at a distance, acknowledged but denied as 'bad', and therefore unattainable for exploration.

'I used to imagine him dead, and sometimes, even myself killing him. What it would be like to stick a knife into him, and how I'd say it was an accident... And then I'd feel so guilty: "thou shalt not kill" '.

Here there was a long pause, and I had no idea of where Maura had gone in her head. She had allowed her rage to surface briefly, but her guilt had also surfaced, and I waited to see if she could allow the release of this anger, both from long ago and of today. The moment passed, and she moved sideways again.

'And when I think about it now, maybe it's no big deal. The papers are full of much worse cases, and when I read about them, it brings it all back. And anyway I can't remember a lot of it.'

Maura appeared to be distancing herself somewhat from the pain and sadness of the last session. Sometimes clients who reach deep into their hidden selves to do a particularly painful and intense piece of work in a session, will retreat, and perhaps not appear at all for the next session, or will come but use it to discuss safer topics. Being aware of this possibility allows me to be with my client in her withdrawal, hoping it is only temporary, and recognising how difficult it is to re-enter an area of pain, and possibly acknowledging this with her.

The client needs to check out my attitude after such revelations, and reassure herself that my positive regard has not changed. It is important that I convey my acceptance of this client, because while it is unlikely that I will be critical or condemnatory, to be overprotective or overly sympathetic would be as potentially damaging to my client's already poor self-image.

'It's difficult to remember, and the bits that do come back are so painful that you try to forget them again?'

This is a time for reflecting feelings, *and* adding something, some intuitive insight. Very often this is accurate, but not always, so it is good to offer it as a possibility, rather than as a stated fact or a certainty. At this stage in the relationship, the counsellor knows enough of the client's story, and her possible reactions, to make such guesses, but at the beginning of a relationship, it is sufficient to reflect back the feelings for confirmation.

'Yes, and I feel so guilty. He wasn't so much older than me and… and… a bit of me enjoyed it (in a whisper). So I must have been to blame too.'

And Maura kept her eyes from mine, as if afraid to read how I might be reacting. I was tempted to ask how a six-year-old could be guilty, but her shame around the physical enjoyment needed to be acknowledged.

'I know that even when we're small we can be aroused and stimulated, like we react when we're tickled. You still feel guilty about this, as if you'd done something wrong or bad?'

Maura's relief was almost tangible. By responding in a matter of fact way to what she considered to be deeply shameful and hateful in herself, I was again able to illustrate my unchanged positive regard for her, and to enable her to look clearly at her experience and reactions, without the distorting fog of shame and guilt.

'I never thought of it like that. I always thought I must have wanted it on some level. And then I was ashamed of making love with my husband. It always seemed somehow dirty, and I couldn't tell him. I couldn't talk about sex at all, so we just did it, and it wasn't much fun for either of us. We used to get on quite well, but the physical side was a disaster. I wasn't surprised when he found someone else.'

She paused, then continued:

'I remember in school about that time, my best friend moved away, and I can't remember having real friends again. I always felt somehow different, that I had to hide, and it's all a blur. I feel as if a large part of me has disappeared, and I'd like to find out about it.'

I sensed a huge history of loss when Maura looked back at her life: loss of childhood, of friends, of marriage, and now even loss of memories.

'You'd like to be able to remember more, and perhaps we can look back together during the next session.'

And look back we did, for several and many sessions more. I encouraged Maura to image herself in her home, room by room, and look at the flashes of recall, of emotions, of people, of happenings. She brought in photos of herself as a child, and shared them with me, and wept over them, as the childhood self echoed through her adult self, demanding a voice after so many years. She reclaimed her childhood, and began to reintegrate her divided selves, her adult person and her small child self. Her self-knowledge grew as she began to see herself whole, and to retrace the experiences that had gone towards making the person she was today.

## Session 53

By Session 53, Maura was beginning to be more confident in herself, and in her actions and decisions. This session began with Maura looking at how terrifying her home had been, with no safety from her abuser. She had shared a lot about her parents, and I had a picture of a distracted and somewhat cold mother, and a workaholic father, who had no time for either his children or his wife. Having always been told 'to get on with it', whether it was a cut knee or trouble at school, she had moved to believing that her parents knew about the uncle's abuse ('grown-ups know everything') and that she was being punished by them for something unknown, or for just being a 'very bad' person. She painted a picture of a small child creeping around the house, always afraid and always wary, lest worse befall her.

'There doesn't appear to have been anywhere safe for you?'

I did not think this was particularly forceful, or even a particularly wise statement, but it acted as a trigger for Maura.

'Of course there wasn't. Haven't I been telling you? Is that all you can say – that it wasn't safe? It was terrifying, it was monstrous. I'm afraid even to allow myself to think about it. Are you listening at all?'

It would have been easy here to insist that I had been listening, that there was no need to attack me. Instead, I managed to remain aware that it was a measure of the current safety in the relationship that Maura felt able to allow her anger against the world to surface in the form of rage against me.

'It's easy for you, sitting there comfortably. But it isn't easy being me. I used to look at my children, and wonder how anyone could let a child be so miserable and so afraid.'

I was aware that Maura was close to tears, as so often happens after such an outburst, and that in her weeping her anger would dissolve and retreat and turn back into helplessness, so I encouraged her to stay with it:

'You'd like to tell your parents just how bad it was?'

And Maura's anger flared again, and in no uncertain terms she poured out what she would have liked, and would like even now, to say to them. The focus for the rage had shifted from her abuser to her parents, who had so visibly failed to protect her, to do their job as parents, and with such disastrous results for Maura. I sat with her, aware of how easy it would be for me to join in her rage against her mother and father, to take upon myself her perception of their behaviour, and also aware of my painful appreciation of how bad it had been for the small Maura, and how much she was suffering today. I needed to place this concern to one side, because right now Maura needed me to be with her in *her* anger.

After a time, Maura faded into silence, and looked at me aghast.

'How awful. I feel so guilty saying these things. But I'm relieved to have said them. I think I've wanted to say them for years. What must you think of me?'

And she did weep now, sobbing and unrestrained, so different from the silent painful tears of earlier sessions. She wept like a child, with her whole self, and I could sense the relief.

I felt it was important to be aware of the great risk Maura was taking in dismantling her childhood defences. She was challenging her childhood illusions of absolute safety and absolute love existing somewhere, if only she could find them or access them. She now needed to learn new coping skills for these new situations, by constructing new models of partial goodness, of diluted affection, of relationships which are punishing and rewarding at the same time.

As counsellors, we recognise the confusion between past and present realities, and share that recognition with the client. We need to respond to two different realities which contradict one another: the intensity of the childhood reality, which no longer really exists, but according to whose rules the client may still be operating, and the diffused adult reality, perhaps only glimpsed in the mind. As adults, both realities can exist simultaneously within us, and we need to test these, by taking a risk that discriminates one from the other. The important thing is not to give in to the urge to retreat to our childhood way of being, but to be ready to learn from the new experience.

'It's very painful looking at how unhappy you were, but I sense you feel less helpless now, as if a load had shifted from your shoulders, and you feel sad but less weighed down.'

Remembering and presenting earlier statements can be valuable at any time in counselling, but just now, I actually felt Maura looked less burdened. And indeed she stretched her arms, a freer gesture than she normally made, and said yes, she was able to leave now, and felt she was leaving some of her trouble behind her.

## Session 68

Over the next few sessions Maura was angry and sad in turn, grieving the loss of both her childhood and also the loss of her unreal expectations of perfection and her image of parents who would, one day, rescue her. She was beginning to see and to accept the frightening prospect that she was her own rescuer and her own protector. She had come when the task of maintaining these illusions proved too great, when the energy needed to prop these up was no longer available, and when the precipitating events of the reappearance of her abuser, the increase in reporting of abuse cases in the media, and the loss of her children's childhood when they moved out, all combined to flood her with old emotions, to the point where she could no longer cope effectively with everyday life. Much of our counselling work had been the effort to recognise and to accept that this inability to cope caused overload, but that new and more realistic and effective skills can be learned. If the client can recognise this pattern, and learn from it, then she can, to some extent, be her own counsellor in the future.

In Session 68, Maura brought new material with her.

'I've now lost the only friend I had. It's not easy for me to make friends, but this woman works with me, and we go out and about quite a bit together. We get on well, and we have good laughs together. And now she says she'll never speak to me again.'

'Tell me about it.'

'We had a row over a silly film. I made the mistake of saying anyone who liked that kind of filth wasn't normal, and she said she'd seen it and enjoyed it, and did I think she was abnormal? She shouted at me and went off, so that's that. I'll never see her again.'

'You really feel she's gone for good.'

'Yes. I wish I'd never said anything about that wretched film. I really hated it, but I should have shut up and gone along with her. I usually don't let out my opinions, just hear what she has to say, and agree... Now I've really blown it and it's all my fault. I'm stupid.'

And she cried quietly.

It would be easy here to launch into a lecture about having a right to her own opinion about the state of modern films, about her friend not being worth it anyway if that's all it took to chase her away. And the client could go away, still without her friend, but with her feelings of being stupid and out of step increased. It was more important to help her to explore her idea that friendship was one-sided, her sadness at having fought with her friend, her belief that friendship demands constant sweetness and light and cannot survive a disagreement, her lack of trust in her own opinions, and what she really means by the word 'stupid' and where she first heard it applied to herself.

'Tell me about her.'

And Maura talked about her friend, and the good times

137

they'd had together, and her belief that this had now all irretrievably vanished, for ever, finally. Her sense of absolutes was surfacing here again. If it wasn't perfect, then it was disaster.

'I remember that you lost a friend when you were seven because she moved away. Perhaps you feel this friend has also gone away for good?'

It seemed to me to be important to identify her sense of loss as being both current, but also echoing the childhood misery when her friend left her lonely, when she particularly needed her. By linking these episodes, and moving to her expectations of being let down, and to her attempts to be other than herself, a false self trying to please everyone else, we explored what it would be like to be angry with someone, and yet remain friendly. This was an idea utterly foreign to Maura. If you had a row, that was that. No going back, no compromise, they would never want to be near you again. Her black-and-white vision of the world, all or nothing, was a childish blueprint for living 'happily ever after' which made her very fearful of any change, of not being in control at all times.

'It reminded me of a dream I had lately. I was in an airport and the place was packed. Lots of people and a great buzz as they talked about their holidays, and where they were going. I could hear them clearly, but they couldn't hear me. And they didn't seem to be able to see me either. And then I realised that I was wearing the invisible hat, and I took it off, but instead of becoming visible to everyone, they all disappeared. And there I was, no one else around, and all these planes coming in to land, or getting ready to take off, and I was the only person who could do anything. It was all down to me to save the day. Then I woke up.'

It is always tempting to interpret someone else's dreams. We assume we can see it as clearly as they can, that their referents match ours, and that perhaps we have superior detachment or insight. It seemed clear to me that the dream reflected effort to communicate, isolation and fear of responsibility, but when I asked Maura what it meant to her, she said how empowered she had felt when she woke up. She thought the dream had highlighted her past efforts to communicate, but now she realised that it was up to her, whether others were speaking or not, and that she was able to survive even such responsibility as the dream seemed to present.

It was then I realised how far Maura had moved from the frightened person who had come to look for help more than a year ago.

## Session 84

During Session 75 I had broached to Maura the idea of ending her work with me. It seemed to me that she had gained sufficient insight into herself and how she operated and reacted to events and people, to be able now to launch out on her own as her own guide and planner. Initially she reacted with panic, querying her readiness and her fear of being 'cast adrift'. I had asked that we discuss the idea of ending, rather than making a statement of ending, which would perhaps have been too directive for Maura, and which might have felt to her like being dismissed. I was clear about leaving the choice of ending to her, and she savoured this new strength in her, perceived by me, to make her own decisions. She was making a free choice, to stay longer or to leave, and it seemed to be a vote of confidence by us both in her readiness to take responsibility for that decision, right or wrong.

The time we had spent discussing the abuse, with its attendant feelings of disgust, blame, guilt and rage, had formed the core of our work, but it had by no means been the only focus. We had looked at this as a traumatic event in her life, but one which she had survived and which she had now used to explore her complex self and to get to know herself better.

'I think what I'm most angry, and sad about, is the childhood I have lost, and indeed the marriage I might have saved if I had looked for help earlier. But who knows? I'm not going to lose any more time. I feel somehow in charge now, and while I know it's not all going to be plain sailing, I feel I'll be able to struggle on. I'm hoping to go on holiday abroad soon, and I know I couldn't have done that last year. Not on my own.'

Reviewing the progress made over the time spent together is valuable for both client and counsellor, and it can often take several 'ending' sessions rather than just one. It enables the client to look back at the person she was when she first came, full of fear and suppressed rage, and contrast this with the person she now sees herself to be. It also gives the opportunity to look forward to future difficulties of which she can only be dimly aware, but it is important that she acknowledge these.

'I know that I may crumble the next time I go home and see my uncle, but I feel that's OK. I won't stay crumbled. And I'd like to tell my mother and father about what he did, and how I've always blamed them in some way, but they're old and I'm not sure that I will. It might destroy them. But somehow I know that I *can* if I choose to. And knowing that, it doesn't seem as important whether I do or not.'

Maura is no longer fenced around by compulsions and no-go areas. Her awareness of choices, and resultant responsibility, has increased. She is closer to the 'fully functioning person' described by Carl Rogers as being more open to experience, able to live in each moment, trusting in herself rather than in the evaluations of others, more fully aware of her feelings and reactions. She is free to choose, to exercise her 'free will'.[2]

A final session is also the time when the differing agendas of the client and of the counsellor can be accommodated together. For clients, counselling work is a period in their lives when they suffer and learn, and then go on to use that learning. It is a chapter in their lives, firmly based on the previous part, and equally focused on the future chapters. For the counsellor, it is more like a whole piece, illuminated by the client's past, but with a fixed ending. It can be very difficult for the counsellor to remember the fluidity and ongoing nature of the client's agenda for the work, and the temptation can be for the counsellor to look for tidy endings, completed aims, guarantees of change and improvement for the future. The curtain-call is for the counsellor, because the client's drama will continue beyond the closed curtain, but without the counsellor. The counsellor lives without ever (or almost ever) knowing the outcomes of her work. It is like reading books that have the final chapters missing, so ending sessions demand that the counsellor let go gracefully, and for ever. (The occasional client will send a Christmas card, or a holiday card, to update progress, or her progress will filter through from a different source, but this is the exception rather than the rule).

'It feels odd to be talking about not being here. I'll miss coming. And I don't just mean not having this hour allocated every week. I'll... I find this very hard to say... I'll miss you. And yet I don't think I'll be losing you. I almost feel you're lodged in my head, and I find myself saying at tough times, 'What would she say if she were here?' And I can almost hear you. And you're not giving me advice, or saying what to do, but you're saying 'Wait a minute. Stand back. What's really happening here and where are you in all this?' And then I can take a deep breath, and make some decision, or not, as the case may be.'

And I was glad to be able to answer honestly:

'I'll miss you too. I feel we have worked well together and you've been generous in sharing of yourself. I'm glad to hear you've found it so beneficial. If you feel at any time in the future that you'd like to undertake further work, I do hope you'll get in touch. And if I were not available, that you'd make some new contact. I do believe it can be helpful.'

Maura rang me the following Christmas to say she was well, to say 'thank you', and to ask how I was. That was our last contact.

### REFERENCES

1. Rogers, Carl, *Client-Centred Therapy* (London: Constable, 1951), p. 51.
2. Kirschenbaum, H. and Henderson, V. Land (eds), *The Carl Rogers Reader* (London: Constable, 1990), p. 416.

# PART III

# CHAPTER 7

## EFFECTS ON THE COUNSELLOR

*A person-centred approach is based on the premise that the
human being is basically a trustworthy organism, capable of
evaluating the outer and inner situation, understanding herself in
its context, making constructive choices as to the next steps in life,
and acting on those choices.*[1]

### Awareness of Self

In the counselling relationship, there are two people involved
and therefore the interactions will affect both.

A high level of self-awareness is required, both for the
protection of the counsellor and for the benefit of the client. If
I do not have an acute awareness of myself and of my reactions
to the words, moods and emotions of others, I can take on the
depression and fears of my clients.

> If we are unable to look after ourselves it is unlikely that
> we will have much of substance to offer to others.[2]

I need to be constantly striving to remain aware of the divide
between my client and myself, between my feelings and his,
between my perceptions and his. The line between empathy and
being engulfed by the client's emotional world is a thin one,
which needs to be constantly patrolled. It demands that we
somehow manage to enter the client's world, while still keeping
a foot in our own. Without this foothold or connection, we
could be swept away in our involvement in our client's
emotions, and then we would cease to be of help, and become
merely a fellow-traveller in an emotional jungle.

> Therapists have a dual role: they must both observe and participate in the lives of their patients…. As participant, one enters into the life of the patient and is affected and sometimes changed by the encounter.[3]

As counsellors, we need somehow to retain a link into our own world, our own persons, and not become absorbed and lost in the world of the client. This level of detachment can be difficult, as it appears to militate against effective empathy. It is an attempt not to become over-involved, to aim for non-attachment, without merely saying 'do not get involved'. If our contact with our client is spontaneous, and if we empty ourselves of our own concerns for the time of the session, then we can retain the focus on the client, without ever fully extinguishing the light on ourselves. We can switch our attention from ourselves, and yet remain always aware of ourselves. If we can be aware of our separateness as client and counsellor, then we can move without fear into the close relationship of counselling. Our aim is to be separate but together, involved without becoming enmeshed, balanced in the shared experience of the work.

It is difficult to remember that clients are observing us, noting what we do or say, assessing us and our interactions, trying to get to know us and the effect we have on them, positive or negative.

> Every analyst and therapist communicates far more to the patient about himself than is usually realised.[4]

By our transparency or congruence, we try to be open and visible to our clients, but we can never know how they compare us to others, or how they match our selves to their inner pictures, so we can be continually surprised when they share with us a glimpse of how they perceive us. This highlights our need to be comfortable and confident in ourselves, irrespective of whether a client sees us as an omnipotent problem-solver, a disinterested observer, or a kind helper. Not only can we never really know, but the client himself may not really know how he views us, never having closely examined the relationship, and he may also change his opinion day by day. The client's picture is the client's *perception* of us, as we impact on him in the relationship.

In *Cry Hard and Swim* by Jacqueline Spring, she describes herself as a client becoming aware one fine afternoon that her counsellor was spending the next couple of hours at a football match. Initially she felt life was unfair, because she was left to suffer while her therapist would be able to enjoy a match without reference to her. And then her feeling changed:

> I had no responsibility for her (the therapist). She cared deeply for me, but she wasn't going home to worry about me. 'I could look after myself' – she trusted my ability to do so. She didn't need me, depend on me, expected nothing from me.[5]

The nature of their work together changed, becoming deeper as the client realised she could tell this counsellor, whom she cared for greatly, of even the worst moments of her life, and she would not be burdened or injured by her revelations. On another occasion, seeking to balance the heaviness and dread in her inner world:

> I was scared stiff I might see her emotionally affected… I needed her objectivity more than anything.[6]

The reality is that, as we love and respect our clients, they may also love and respect us, and wish not to burden us, nor to shock or disgust us. This is partly because they fear we might turn from them in disapproval or distaste, but also because they do not wish to hurt us. The client needs to be aware of our ability to hear, absorb and yet remain detached from whatever they reveal, and also our ability to remain focused on the inner self of the client, without being distracted by the outer facts.

One of the most fearful aspects of counselling for the trainee counsellor (and indeed often for the experienced counsellor also) is that there is no way of knowing in advance what material is going to be presented by the client, or what manner of person is going to come to a first session.

The counsellor will never meet two exactly similar people, with the same reactions and background responses to a given situation. Even if the situations, and all the outlined material – age, sex, marital status, children, job, upbringing – sound exactly the same, the life experience and emotional reactions will be entirely different. It follows, therefore, that there are no learned responses, no catch-all phrases behind which we can hide. The counsellor has no tried and tested solutions or antidotes, but works with and responds to each client in the moment, using the client's material, responding imaginatively and creatively, striving to understand and to reflect that understanding, maintaining a calmness in the maelstrom of the client's emotional expression.

> …the capacity to tolerate uncertainty is a prerequisite for the profession.[7]

### Sitting with the Uncertainty

We all feel more comfortable with certainties, and if we are in unknown territory, we look for a map and a guide. In the person-centred approach to counselling, our guide is the client, troubled, confused, fearful. The temptation can be to cling to theory or technique to achieve some certainty for ourselves, or to produce a solution to some aspect of the client's dilemma.

This time of not-knowing can be difficult to sustain when a client is demanding direction:

> 'You must know. You are the counsellor. You are the expert. I'm stuck and I don't know what to do or where to turn.'

It requires courage as a counsellor to admit to not knowing, to oneself, or to the client. We too feel stuck in the face of the client's fear and confusion. 'What now? I must do/say something. I'm hopeless, I'm failing this client.' Patience is needed, and also infinite resources of self.

A willingness to sit with the unknown until something new or different emerges, or until the client can perhaps explore his difficulty in coping with a sense of uncertainty, can result in some of the more obviously defining moments in counselling.

> Therapists sometimes have to tolerate extended periods during which they may feel ignorant and helpless.[8]

It is as if our work linked into the human condition, aware of and acknowledging the uncertainty of human designs and plans, and stated firmly, 'we work in this together, we explore your world as it is, and we will move forward as your condition and abilities dictate'. If therapists:

> ...can bear the strain of not-knowing, they can learn that their competence as therapists includes a capacity to tolerate feeling ignorant or incompetent, and a willingness to wait (and to carry on waiting) until something genuinely relevant and meaningful begins to emerge.[9]

From this confusion and 'stuckness', the client often identifies a core point or hitherto unseen direction, as if by listening closely to the confusion, it becomes a background noise, out of which rises the note of the important next step. This requires trust in the process, and a belief in the basic theory of Rogers, that in the climate created by the three core conditions offered by the counsellor, the client will begin to be able to accept himself as the counsellor accepts him, and will become free to change and grow. Within this process, it becomes possible to sit in the uncertainty, believing that this unknowing is a part of the work, which will proceed towards awareness and self-knowledge and acceptance on the part of the client. It is necessary to have been part of the unfolding process in order to fully accept it and believe it, but no matter how often we prove the resulting effectiveness, waiting can still cause anxiety and stress in us as counsellors.

These 'stuck' moments are part of the attempt to facilitate the client to change by 'freeing the natural healing process within the client'.[10] The inclination may be to suggest or encourage some course of action, any movement being less uncomfortable than this feeling of helplessness. The danger here is not merely that we will be 'problem-solving', but also that our attempt may be heard as 'I will continue to respect and accept you *if* (and only if) you now move in this or that direction'.

Clients can choose to stay with the unhappy familiar rather than take the risk of looking at change. Having found a way of surviving, even if it is fearful and watchful, they believe it works for them, and certainly it is familiar. There is no guarantee that a new and different way of operating will be successful, and it might even result in disintegration. The unknown can sometimes be so frightening that clients will admit that they wish to go no further, that they choose not to risk change.

Clients sometimes leave therapy and choose to stay in an

abusive relationship, because the unfamiliar is even more frightening than familiar abuse.

As counsellors, we need to believe fully in the possibility of change. Phrases such as 'It's in her nature' or 'All his family is like that. What can you expect?', have in common a belief in the immutability of personality traits. They suggest that it is impossible for people to change their behaviours and attitudes through exploration and awareness and decisions. Such certainty is often put forward as a denial of responsibility for actions and reactions: 'I couldn't help it. I had no choice. That's the way I am'. The process of change begins with an awareness of the way I am or the way I behave, acknowledging this, and then beginning to explore other ways of being or behaving, choosing or deciding to change in a specific way. It is the wish to change or to be different that brings clients into counselling, and it is the achieving of this change that leads them towards ending therapy. If from the start a counsellor were to consider a client too set in his ways, too old, too distant, too frivolous, the work would have little hope of being successful.

**Transferred Feelings**

The provision of a safe relationship, within which the client ventures to examine and explore his other relationships, is the aim of the Person-Centred Approach. In chapter 3 we looked at how the client may transfer feelings from other sources on to the person of the counsellor, and how the counsellor in turn may be affected, thus colouring her response to the client. As in any relationship, the client and counsellor will react emotionally to one another, and the infantile attitudes can be transferred inappropriately. Rogers refers to these as 'transferential attitudes'.

Rogers also believed that it is not logical to assume that a response which duplicates a prior similar response is of necessity *replicating* it. Feelings of liking or resentment by the counsellor can be reactions to attitudes or behaviours of the client, or they can be feelings which have no relation to the behaviour or person of the client, but are transferred from their original and real origin within the counsellor. They can also be feelings experienced by the counsellor in response to feelings expressed by the client towards the counsellor. Whichever they may be (and it can be difficult to sort out their origin), the congruent counsellor will allow these feelings into awareness and acknowledge these to herself. If necessary, or if she deems it helpful to the client, she will use these in the relationship. The bringing of these feelings and reactions into the open frees the counsellor from the need to prevaricate, to avoid certain areas of discussion, and releases her to become again the real and transparent person the relationship demands. It reassures the client that he is working with such a person, who is in effect modelling how we can be in relationships, without masks or defences, but real in the moment. The client is searching for his real self, and who will offer him a true mirror where he can glimpse this? Perhaps the counsellor can, by being aware of her own feelings and moving through and beyond these. The use of the counsellor's whole person, openly and honestly, is what makes this relationship unique and uniquely helpful.

## Boundaries

Boundaries in the counselling relationship are both external and internal, and are put in place for the benefit of both the client and the counsellor. The establishment of these will meet the professional requirements of the counsellor, and all aspects can be discussed and agreed with the client. Without such agreements, the counsellor will be trying to work without any safeguards for herself, without the support of some practical certainties, burdened by the worries of constant small decisions.

A client could feel free to change appointments, come late and try to stay longer, phone at inappropriate times, and generally render the counsellor powerless to protect herself in any way.

For the client, boundaries enable him to get a picture of how the work will progress, to remain in some control of procedures. They enhance the aspect of safety and allay fears of the unexpected, and give some guarantee of consistency and equality in the relationship. Clients who are accustomed to relinquishing totally any control in medical or legal matters, may bring something of the same response to counselling, and awareness of boundaries can render the experience less threatening, especially at the start. It is the responsibility of the counsellor to set and maintain these boundaries, as the client, being new to this work, is probably unaware of the need for these safeguards, of confidentiality, time, money, etc.

### Boundaries of Time

It is essential that a client knows the precise time of an appointment and the duration of a session. Clear statements about an appointment at ten o'clock, lasting for one hour, form a basis on which the counsellor can build a picture of herself as a dependable and trustworthy person. If the counsellor is late for an appointment, it can give an impression of lack of respect for the client, and it can create anxiety in the client as to whether this person can be relied on in what she says. If the time of a session is fixed at an hour, the client needs to know that this does not mean ten minutes less because I have another appointment, or fifteen minutes extra because I have nothing else to do. It can be difficult for a client to stand up and say 'I must go. I have another appointment'.

If a client arrives late, it is important to maintain the time of ten to eleven o'clock, even if the client has missed twenty minutes of this. The message is that the counsellor will be there for the time specified whether the client can be there or not. It offers a picture of security, that this is the client's time, and that while the counsellor keeps her word, she is not available at all hours. Above all, the message conveyed is that the counsellor is taking the client seriously, trusting him and giving him the responsibility to enter into a relationship or not. It gives a point of stability and certainty in what is often a world of chaos. The maintenance of the boundary of one hour for a session, if that is what was agreed, allows the client the safety of knowing just how much time remains in a session, and gives him the ability to disclose or not disclose material at any given time. The counsellor needs to have a clock within her sight, but the client also benefits from knowing what time remains.

### *Boundaries of Money*

There must be a clear agreement from the start about payment for sessions, the amount, the form (whether credit cards are acceptable), and if the counsellor requires the client to pay for sessions cancelled with less than twenty-four hours' notice (this is becoming standard practice for many counsellors). Some counsellors find it difficult to ask for money at the end of a session, particularly if a client is not well-off, or they find the actual handling of money and giving change distasteful. As counsellors, we need to be clear in our minds about being paid for the service we offer, or we may transmit our unease to clients who may be anxious to pay their way. It is of course easier if we work for a counselling centre, where we can put the onus of being paid on the centre, but generally it is an area where we need to consider our philosophy and be clear about how we see our service. I believe it is important for a client to pay a fee, no matter how small, for counselling sessions. This ensures that the client can feel 'in charge' of the sessions, free to criticise the service, to be angry or to disagree with the counsellor. If sessions are perceived as being 'a charity', free time in some way donated by a patronising counsellor, it is much more difficult to promote equality in the relationship. It maintains visible respect for the client if the counsellor believes that he wishes to be treated as able and willing to pay, and it maintains the client's respect for the process as being real and valuable rather than a handout. Once these attitudes are established, then special circumstances can be discussed or a sliding scale can be arranged.

### Boundaries of Confidentiality

Counsellors need to be fully aware of their stance on the issue of confidentiality, or else each client will impact in different ways and the result will be ongoing worries and uncertainties, and attempts to fit confidentiality, whether partial or absolute, into the framework of different clients.

In the same way as the heart of the counselling relationship is mutual trust, so the heart of that trust must be the guarantee of confidentiality. Is this guarantee absolute? To start with, there is no demand on the client to maintain this confidentiality, and clients do discuss with friends and relations the form and contact of the counselling sessions and relationship. We often hear, 'I was talking to my sister about the last session, and she agrees that...'. And we wonder what impression of us as counsellors is being passed on to someone else, or how much the client's reported perception of a session would compare with our memory of that same session. Some counsellors request confidentiality from their clients when they share a personal experience with that client, and group counselling demands confidentiality from its members.

The guarantee of absolute secrecy, from the counsellor's point of view, can also be subject to certain limitations.

At the initiation of the service, the counsellor must

discuss the limits of confidentiality with the client. The right of the client to privacy is relative. It is not absolute. It is subject to the constraints resulting from other rights and values held by society.[11]

These constraints include: potential danger or damage to another person, through violence or drug supply; abuse, physical or sexual, of a child, which, in Ireland, may shortly be subject to mandatory reporting by a counsellor; reports prepared for legal purposes on behalf of a client whose counselling sessions are being paid for by the courts and are part of his conditions of bail or probation; disclosures directly affecting a school or institution that has employed a counsellor to work with its students; information apparently vital to the medical or psychiatric condition of a client, who is being looked after by a medical team which includes a counsellor; material shared with a third party or group for the purposes of ongoing supervision for the counsellor or student/trainee counsellor.

There are many more areas where confidentiality can be seen as less than absolute, but it is not likely that any one client will be subject to many of these special circumstances. What is important is that the client be notified if at all possible, in advance, of these limitations which apply to his particular case, and if further limitations on confidentiality arise during the sessions, that the client be told, as soon as possible, of these. Even if such notification were to terminate the counselling relationship, or limit it in some way, respect for the client demands that such knowledge is fully shared.

Counsellors use statements such as 'I would like to assure you that confidentiality is guaranteed, except where the safety or well-being of a third party is concerned. If that should arise, I might be bound to report such dangers elsewhere'. Many counsellors include statements about the safety or harming of the client herself, the identity of who would be informed in the event of reporting, or the proviso that the counsellor would always inform the client prior to such reporting. More detailed information about confidentiality might be required when working with an under-age child brought by her parents, for example, or an employee referred by his employer, who is paying for the counselling sessions.

The legal picture of confidentiality is not clear at this time. There do not appear to be tested precedents for claiming 'privilege' in respect of not disclosing information about a client, if a court of law demands such disclosure. However, 'Successful pleas have been made to retain confidentiality of the counselling content' and 'it is essential that every possible alternative avenue be explored before the decision to break confidentiality is made'.[12]

Open and frank discussion with the client on ongoing aspects of confidentiality and resulting decisions are equally essential. Whatever the consequences of such openness, the client must be treated with respect and trust, and empowered to make his own decisions in the light of the counsellor sharing such concerns.

## Boundaries of Physical Contact

The question of whether or not touch may be used effectively in the counselling relationship is the subject of much debate. Opinions range from a willingness to hug and to comfort clients in response to a client's wish for physical contact, to a firm resolve that physical contact of any kind whatsoever has absolutely no place in the counselling relationship. As in so many other areas, perhaps the golden mean is the answer. It is important that the counsellor be comfortable with touch and with contact, and she can then make the decision whether or not to embrace a client, or how to react if the client initiates a sudden hug. It is important that the counsellor explore for herself her issues around physical contact, and that she have made her own decisions on how to react before such contact takes place. Personal space can differ so much from person to person, that it is never safe to assume that a hug means the same to a client as to a counsellor. To many people, a hug is the same as a handshake, but to others it is a personal invasion.

As counsellor, I do not instigate physical contact. It could be difficult for a client to reject my gesture, it could be embarrassing if I had misread the situation, it could be awkward if my client is not comfortable with his own physical presence, it could be misconstrued if a client had any sexual attraction towards me. As I sat once with a client in great distress, reliving an episode of abuse, I felt so intensely for her that I reached across and touched her hand, thinking I would reassure her that she was not on her own. To my surprise, she and her chair shot violently backwards. I had interpreted my own distress and need for comfort, as hers. The last thing she needed right then was any physical contact, and her reaction was immediate. From this I learned to be more aware of how I can be affected by my client's pain. I interrupted her work by appearing to say: 'I cannot bear to see you suffering, so I will try to rescue you'. If my client says she is lonely and how much she needs to be held and comforted, and were I to respond and embrace her, then I feel I would be rescuing her, and helping to cut her off from the sadness which she has finally contacted. Her future work would be stunted, because whenever she was in touch with that unhappiness, she would look outside for resolution, rather than to her own resources within. She needs to acknowledge the pain, and experience it fully, recognise its origins and learn to lessen or counteract it in her own way.

Of course I will suffer with my client, as I sit with her, but this is part of the task of the counsellor. Years ago I was told,

'You must not deny another person their right to suffering', and I did not understand, but now I think this is what was meant. We each need to recognise and experience the impact of events on us, and use this impact to grow and become the person we can be.

### Boundaries of Personal Information

Boundaries of relationship, or personal boundaries, are difficult to define with certainty, and different counsellors have different rules for their practice.

For me, being congruent allows me to share personal details at times, and to decline to share at other times. 'I had a great holiday, thank you. The weather was beautiful. And how have you been?' answers the client's question, acknowledges that he knew I was away on holidays, confides that it was a good holiday, and quickly returns the focus to where it belongs, on the client. Lengthy descriptions of sun and sea, and missed travel connections, are quite out of place. This is, after all, the client's hour.

If a client asks me a personal question, I have the choice as to whether I respond or not. If asked, 'Are you married?', I will respond 'Yes I am' or 'I was but now I'm separated' or whatever is true, and immediately re-focus on the client. I may draw attention to some words used just before the question, or I may try to discover if the asking of the question was significant for the client. Some counsellors refuse to divulge anything whatsoever of their private lives, believing that to do so alters the balance of the holding relationship, but I believe that to remain a cypher may raise fantasies or imaginings. It is also possible that the counsellor could give a different picture of being evasive, or secretive, or even mysterious.

If my client were to ask some question which I did not wish to answer, I would like to be able to respond in such a way that acknowledged the question, the client's right to ask it, and my right not to answer it. 'How much money do you earn as a counsellor?'; 'I feel that is not something I'm willing to disclose' or 'I don't wish to answer that question'. This is an honest refusal to give information that I feel is private, but it is not a denial of the client's right to ask it if he wishes, nor a re-direction of the question like a boomerang, back to the client. It could be followed by, 'I'm not sure why this is important to you right now?', but I like to state whether or not I'm happy to answer the query in the first instance.

A student once reported, in horrified tones, that a client had kissed his hand as she left a session. On exploration, it transpired that the client was an elderly woman who would have grown up in an atmosphere where such a kiss would have had respectful and religious connotations, rather than the abject self-abasing image the young student had presumed. Once this had been acknowledged, the student was able to discuss his client's gesture with her, without conveying his initial shock. He explained that his role was as facilitator rather than a solver of problems, and that he saw her as doing the work and being responsible for the outcome, and how he saw her kiss as a possible sign of dependence on him as an expert. It was an important point of growth in the relationship.

Relationship boundaries can be threatened in a small town where everyone seems at times to know everyone else, or in an area where half the population appears to be related to the other half! Meeting a client in a public place, for example at a funeral, could place a burden on the client to 'explain' the counsellor to others who do not know he is coming for help. On these occasions, it is wise to leave acknowledgement of the acquaintance to the client. If he appears stricken at the sight of the counsellor, it is possible to go along with his decision to maintain that he has never met the counsellor before. If it becomes apparent during sessions that the client and the counsellor frequent the same office or pub, then the counsellor can discuss with the client the likelihood of a chance meeting, and whether or not the client would wish to acknowledge their acquaintance.

Meeting clients in the supermarket or the Post Office can create difficulty, particularly if a client were to approach enthusiastically, saying 'Remember what I said to you about my wife? Well, it's all changed and wait till I tell you...'. The counsellor will explain at once that she is not willing to discuss the client's affairs in a public place, and that they will meet at their next session. It is far better to be forthright than to make excuses about being in a hurry.

### Sexual Boundaries

In the warm, safe atmosphere of the counselling relationship, it is not surprising that the positive interaction between client and counsellor can grow towards a more sexual form of attraction, whether on the part of the client or the counsellor, or indeed involving both.

If a client becomes sexually attracted to a counsellor, it is expected that the counsellor will be able to accept that this is so, accept the client in the same non-possessive, non-judgemental way as before, and discuss this openly with the client. There is no reason why the counselling relationship should end, provided that the client wishes to continue, having voiced his feelings, and that the counsellor remains at ease and balanced within herself. If the counsellor can comfortably work with this new development, then it can be a most rewarding experience for the client, to be able to discuss sexual feelings within the reality of a safe relationship. In the unlikely event of such disclosure causing confusion or embarrassment on the part of the counsellor, then perhaps the client would benefit more from a change of therapist.

If the sexual attraction is on the part of the counsellor, and if this cannot be held in awareness without expression, then it will be better brought into the here and now, and shared because not to share it would be an obstacle between client and counsellor in the relationship. This risks the immediate departure of the client, unable to deal with the counsellor in this new guise, but would be preferable to the continuation of a relationship skewed by the counsellor struggling distractedly with an unspoken attraction.

However, to allow sexual attraction to progress to a sexual relationship is quite a different matter. It is useless to deny that this happens, but statistics about its prevalence are very varied. Nevertheless, the balance of power in the counselling relationship is so finely balanced, and so open to being tilted in favour of the counsellor, that it would be very difficult, if not impossible, to tease out how much of the attraction would be the fulfilling of a personal need in the counsellor, rather than a real caring for the other. Generally counselling is undertaken for the benefit of the client; at times it works for the benefit of both client and counsellor; but if it becomes focused solely on the good of the counsellor, then it ceases to be 'good practice'.

> I do not myself believe that it is ethically responsible for a therapist to behave in a way which is solely for his own benefit.[13]

The Code of Ethics of both the Irish Association for Counselling and Therapy (IACT) and the British Association for Counselling (BAC) state that counsellors and therapists should not be involved with their clients in friendship, formal business relationship, sexual or training relationship, while the counselling is current. These codes also spell out the rules about sexual relationships with former clients, and state clearly that the counsellor is accountable if such relationships are entered into. The expectation is that at least two years should elapse after the counselling relationship ends before beginning a sexual relationship. There is a clear recognition of the power located in the client-counsellor relationship, and how this could be abused by the therapist.

Generally, the setting and maintaining of boundaries are essential for the client's awareness of being in a safe and consistent relationship, where the counsellor is capable of holding the client in every conceivable circumstance, of place, of time, of emotional stress and lack of certainty, while at the same time maintaining her own identity boundaries, which are essential for her well-being and protection. While it is the responsibility of the counsellor to set and maintain boundaries, it is essential that the client also be aware of these boundaries. Only then can the work of counselling proceed in safety.

### Supervision

It is only in fairly recent years that supervision has come to be seen as an essential component in the work of responsible practitioners. Regular supervision is now a requirement for becoming an accredited member of both the Irish Association for Counselling and Therapy and the British Association for Counselling, and supervision occupies a central position in the curricula of training courses. It is an acknowledgment that counsellors, like all professionals, can become blinded by the routine, the repetition, of aspects of their work, and since the relationship is central, the counsellor can become too caught up in the process while unaware of her own reactions.

> Counselling is a private activity and supervision is the main, and possibly the only, way that the counselling profession can monitor the work of its members and

endeavour to ensure a competent and ethical service to the public.[14]

The task of the supervisor therefore is not only to protect clients from possible lacunae in the counsellor's work, but also to assist the counsellor in her personal development, in her reactions to the engagement with clients, and above all, to provide a keener focus on both client and counsellor. Supervision is not counselling. The relationship between counsellor and supervisor has many elements in common with the counselling relationship, but it also has differences. The personal developmental work of the counsellor is not the focus. Rather, it is an overview of the client's story and present difficulties, seen through the eyes of the counsellor, and interpreted through the filters of the counsellor's background, current emotional state, and reactions to this particular client. The *raison d'être* of supervision is to help 'clients by helping their counsellors'; it aims 'to promote effective counselling by assisting counsellors in their professional development'.[15]

Supervision takes place either in one to one sessions, or in group sessions. The client's welfare is paramount, and the client's material will be confidential as far as possible (names and identifying characteristics will be omitted).

The relationship between the counsellor and the supervisor is fundamentally important to the effectiveness of the supervisory work, and is characterised by trust. Trust is a two-way component in supervision. The supervisor trusts that the counsellor/supervisee will report honestly and will try to hear what the supervisor is trying to tell her; and the counsellor trusts that the supervisor will be open in her comment and criticism of the work, seeking always to protect the client, to encourage the counsellor, and never to undermine or belittle the counsellor. This relationship will be built slowly, and is open to all the dangers that can occur in a client–counsellor relationship.

The responsibility for effective supervision is shared by both the supervisor and the supervisee. The supervisor is trying to help the supervisee foster her own internal supervisor, her own balanced critic, capable of standing back from her work and objectively seeing what is good, what could be done differently, what could be changed in her work tomorrow. Such an internal supervisor will never replace the value of a supervisor who can see hidden aspects of our work, and of ourselves. Both support *and* challenge are required, and the supervisor can be seen as a kind of gatekeeper, holding open the door of communication between client and supervisee, and allowing the supervisor access to the world of both.

Supervision therefore focuses on the counsellor's self-awareness in the counselling work, and helps to reduce the tension and anxiety which accompanies it. It is essential for the ongoing professional development of the counsellor, and encourages new and creative approaches to the work.

This creative element in supervision can be of great value to the supervisee, allowing for a fresh way of looking at and hearing the client, and a new perspective in what may have become a familiar and over-concentrated picture. 'Two heads are better than one' usually applies in the context of supervision!

## What does the counsellor gain?

In *Beyond Carl Rogers*, Brazier puts forward a persuasive theory that the human being's need to love is as universal and as basic as the need to *be* loved.[16] Rogers had postulated the need in us all to be positively and non-judgementally regarded by others, to be loved unconditionally, for ourselves. The provision of this positive regard by the counsellor is one of the key elements in the relationship, which allows the client to grow and change in safety. Brazier suggests that the need to love others, to care for and to look after others, is at least as basic and as important for our well-being. For the counsellor, therefore, counselling satisfies this need through working with and positively caring for clients, and Brazier believes that this is one of the main reasons why people choose to work as counsellors.[17] He is suggesting that while being nice to others whom we meet may be a way of ensuring that they will positively regard us, we are also good to others because we *need* to be positive towards them. The human person needs both to give and to receive love.

From being an intermittent, part-time activity, perhaps in conjunction with 'the day-job', counselling has become a career. Training courses are more widely available and more wide-ranging in what they offer, and the term 'counsellor' is becoming a job description in its own right. Health Boards, doctors' practices, voluntary bodies, all are currently looking for trained and accredited counsellors. Both the Irish Association for Counselling and Therapy (IACT) and the British Association for Counselling (BAC) have an accreditation system for individual counsellors and for training courses, and reciprocity of accreditation has been agreed between them. This means that standards of training, practice, complaints procedures, and codes of ethics and practice of both organisations are mutually acceptable and binding on members who migrate and set up practice in either country. This growing uniformity of standards, which becomes more demanding each year, is seen by some as a profession closing its ranks to those who are not willing to conform. It is, however, much more the result of a growing awareness that counselling is not something that just happens, something that we read about and apply to others on demand. A grounded knowledge of human psychology and developmental stages is needed if we are to work effectively, and lack of training can not only damage clients but can also have a catastrophic effect on the untrained counsellor, working so closely and intimately with people in psychological distress.

> Whatever my own and others' reservations about the processes of accreditation or licensure, I think this tendency is an inevitability. I believe this is the way of the world and that as a profession we had better 'render unto Caesar' the qualifying hours and tokens he requires... I am wary of a professionalising approach that would give all the power to those peddling and measuring atomistic counselling skills and overlook the need for wisdom and social and spiritual sensitivity.[18]

Feltham offers a cautionary note to counselling associations lest they appear tempted to close ranks or close out those he calls 'effective practitioners', whatever their qualifications, while at the same time he states that '...if the job of counselling is worth doing, it is worth doing well...'[19] The double message is worth hearing: counselling can become a profession, but it is essential that it remain a profession with a heart.

## REFERENCES

1. Kirschenbaum, H. and Henderson, V. Land (eds), *The Carl Rogers Reader* (London: Constable, 1990), p. 382.
2. Cushway, Delia, 'New Directions in Stress' in *New Directions in Counselling*, (eds.) Bayne, Rowan, Horton, Ian and Brimrose, Jenny (London: Routledge, 1996), ch. 13, p. 177.
3. Yalom, Irving D., 'Love's Executioner', *Penguin Psychology*, 1991, p. 13.
4. Casement, Patrick, *On Learning from the Patient* (London: Routledge, 1985), p. 3.
5. Spring, Jacqueline, *Cry Hard and Swim* (London: Virago, 1987), p. 75.
6. Ibid., op. cit., p. 97.
7. Yalom, Irving D., op. cit., p. 13.
8. Casement, Patrick, op. cit., p. 3.
9. Ibid., op. cit., p. 4.
10. Mearns, Dave and Thorne, Brian, *Person-Centred Counselling in Action* (London: Sage, 1988), p. 129.
11. Kennedy, Patricia, 'Confidentiality and the Counselling Profession' in *Éisteach*, vol. 2, no. 2., Autumn 1997, p. 11.
12. Ibid., op. cit., p. 15.
13. Thorne, Brian, 'What are the Boundaries?' in *Therapists' Dilemmas* (ed.) Dryden, Windy (London: Harper and Row, 1985), p. 59.
14. Inskipp, Francesca, 'New Directions in Supervision' in *New Directions in Counselling* (eds.) op. cit., pp. 269-80.
15. Feltham, Colin and Dryden, Windy, *Developing Counsellor Supervision* (London: Sage, 1994), p. x.
16. Brazier, David, 'The Necessary Condition is Love' in Brazier, David (ed.), *Beyond Carl Rogers*, p. 90.
17. Ibid.
18. Feltham, Colin, *What is Counselling?* (London: Sage, 1995), p. 162.
19. Ibid.

# CHAPTER 8

## DIFFERENT METHODS OF COUNSELLING

*At the other end of the scale is the client-centred, experiential,
person-centred approach, consistently stressing the capacity and
autonomy of the person, her right to choose the directions she will
move in her behaviour, and her ultimate responsibility for herself
in the therapeutic relationship, with the therapist's person playing
a real but primarily catalytic part in that relationship.*[1]

### Long- or Short-Term Counselling

Within the last decade, not only has interest in and demand for
counselling increased, but there has also been a notable increase
in concentration on the financial implications of such services
being available to larger numbers of people. While believing
that counselling should be available for all who could benefit
from it, we need to remain aware that this could prove an
expensive addition to our health care provisions.

> Ideally, perhaps, everyone should have access to exactly
> the kind of counselling or therapy they need (however
> long it may take), but realistically this is unlikely ever to
> receive state funding.[2]

Traditionally it has been believed that therapy and change
will take as much time as each individual client needs, and that
it is often likely to be a lengthy process. However, accepting that
different clients require different time spans admits the
possibility and indeed the likelihood that time-limited
counselling does suit some situations. The question is how the
decision is made as to who fits what slot, or what model, and
too often this is on the grounds of cost-effectiveness or

expediency, rather than on whether a long- or short-term approach would suit a particular client.

It is important, but difficult, for practitioners who have always worked in long-term counselling relationships to be open to the possibility that short-term work may be at least as effective in some areas and with some clients. Some studies suggest that the greatest change in clients is apparent after eight sessions in counselling, and that the pace of change diminishes thereafter. However, this 'flight into health' may be the immediate result of relief at finally tackling or disclosing long-concealed difficulties, and may be merely a preparation for a lengthy and painful process of deep-seated change.

The literature on both sides of this debate – long- or short-term counselling work – appears to be quite defensive, as if there were a contest between the two, and perhaps there is! The financial cake is being cut thinner and thinner, and scarce resources have to be spent as best they can. It is also true that traditional long-term methods may appear threatened by the shorter and *seemingly* equally productive briefer contracts, whose proponents may in turn feel they have to prove that their cost-effectiveness is not the only measure of their work or their popularity. Short-term counselling attempts to confine the length of the counselling process to a pre-determined time-span. It aims to alter a client's negative or destructive habits and ways of responding to others by concentrating on problem areas and outlining goals and strategies to solve these. The assumption seems to be that results can be achieved as fast as plans can be made, and it is open to the charge that short-term counselling produces short-term changes only. In the long-term work, time itself is a factor in the outcome, and the premise is that changing *outward* behaviour is not sufficient as lasting change can only be achieved by exploring the underlying motivations, unconscious triggers, perceptions and feelings.

Whatever the differences, it is important that both groups be aware of, and knowledgeable about, each other's methods and motivation. It is not enough for long-term counsellors merely to do the same kind of work as they are accustomed to, but to do less of it, in an acute awareness of a contract of a limited number of sessions. Short-term counselling, in all its manifestations, is a different way of working, and is not just a truncated version of open-ended counselling work. Similarly, counsellors working in a short or limited mode of counselling need to remain aware that further, deeper work may at times be in the best interests of a client. The difficulty of measuring what constitutes long or short in terms of counselling reflects the question: 'How long is a piece of string?'

### Long-term Counselling

In long-term counselling, the needs of the client, together with the perception of progress by both counsellor and client, will dictate both the pace and the length of the work. The altering of feelings and reactions learned over a lifetime cannot be achieved in a few brief hours. Well-founded change takes longer. It is sometimes suggested that, as compared with short-term therapy, there is a lack of focus in the long-term work, and this of course could become the case. However, the person-centred approach is based on Rogers' belief '…that it is the client who knows what hurts, what directions to go, what problems are crucial, what experiences have been deeply buried'.[3] The length of time the work takes will therefore depend on how well or how quickly the client becomes aware of what the 'hurt' is, whether it is currently accessible or buried beneath layers of remembrance, whether it affects more than one area of her life, and how long it then takes for her to discover the remedies or strategies she needs in order to heal, because Rogers also believed that only the client knows these remedies.

Since the person-centred approach to counselling is also based on the belief that the relationship within which the work progresses is crucial to its outcome, the building up of the special relationship will take time, and in the case of a client whose ability to trust has been severely damaged, this time may be long indeed. This trust will dictate how quickly, or how slowly, the client is able to confide and share her exploration of painful issues. Long-buried feelings and strongly defended fantasies do not appear to lend themselves to basic immediate identification or solution, and the confused emotional turmoil of many clients can make the idea of clinically controlled and specifically numbered sessions a difficult match with their distress. Those counsellors who work with an expectation of long-term counselling can of course meet clients who are only prepared to stay for a short number of sessions, and the counsellor works within these confines, explicitly stated by the client. In such cases, the counsellor might offer the possibility of longer work, while remaining totally acceptant of the client's choice.

> Ultimately our belief in the importance of the availability of long-term counselling is an expression of certain values.[4]

These values include a wish to do something thoroughly and slowly rather than in hasty, condensed form, a belief in the importance of the strong and reliable relationship within which to risk change, and a recognition of the fundamental resistance in people to change of any kind. When the goals are not clear, where change is desired without real knowledge of the form of such change, where the habits and ills of a lifetime are being unlearned and new strategies formulated, this cannot be achieved in a hurry.

...long-term counsellors' capacity to bend with the flow of the client's material is not a sign of inadequacy and loss of direction, but sensitive attunement to a changing other with whom a relationship develops.[5]

Six or twelve hours in a life of forty years is too small a component to effect permanent change. Changing foundations takes longer than replacing a roof-tile!

Is there a point in the beginning of our therapeutic alliance when I *know* that this work is going to take a long time? If there is, can I be sure that this is the client's need for time, or my own agenda for perceived healing? A client may leave, despite my conviction that she would benefit greatly from further work, and alternatively I may encourage a client to risk detaching from her dependent attendance, by considering ending the work. A client

...may be lulled into a sense of security by the very ritual of regular appointments. Therapy can become an empty habit, or even a refuge from the real world.[6]

It is important that the counsellor and her supervisor continually question the thrust and the impetus of the work in long-term counselling, ensuring that an element of 'coziness' has not entered in, which could result in the sessions becoming aimless and repetitive. If the work has become slack, and the inner tension of exploration has ceased, then it may be safe, it may be companionable, but progress has ceased. Exploring this with the client could afford an opportunity to check whether there is a deeper level of herself which the client is concealing or avoiding, or to look at the possibility of the client being ready to 'go it alone'. Evaluating the work at intervals offers both client and counsellor an opportunity to stand back and assess progress (or lack of it), and also serves as a reminder that the client is not 'locked in' to a never-ending contract. 'The longer the counselling, the harder it is to be specific about change factors since life circumstances change people and make their influence felt',[7] outside of as well as within the counselling work.

The very closeness and familiarity of the long-term counselling relationship can make it difficult to assess the work honestly, lest inherent criticism be hurtful, and because of the effort to remain objective and detached in this close cooperation. This ties in with a further possibility that the counsellor may '…fall into a habitual way of hearing and relating to the client and hence miss important communications because they are new and unfamiliar'.[8] The counsellor could also prolong the work because it constitutes part of her livelihood, which could in effect be a breach of codes of ethics and practice. These very real possibilities ought to be picked up in supervision, challenged by the supervisor, and resolved one way or the other.

### Short-term Counselling

The temptation is to subscribe to the view that any therapy, however brief, must be beneficial, and this would be hard to prove or disprove. It is, however, obvious that the fragile nature of the defences maintained by some people suggests that concentrated, brief counselling could have a devastating, destabilising effect, and it is not suitable for everyone, any more than long-term counselling is the answer to all the world's unhappiness.

Brief or solution-focused therapy, sometimes elegantly titled 'time-sensitive approaches', emphasises the strengths and competencies of clients rather than focusing on their current deficits. While the search for brief but effective models of counselling is not new, it is within the last decade that interest in short-term counselling has really increased, fuelled in the main by financial considerations, and by the reality of long waiting lists and people needing help *now*. The acknowledgement of the value of counselling, and the awareness of the demand for its provision, has led to a need to spread scarce resources over a wider section of the public. Employee assistance programmes (EAPs) have dramatically increased in industrial and commercial settings, doctors and social services advocate brief counselling work, and the law courts are increasingly encouraging a set number of sessions (currently six) as part of bail or probation conditions.

This short-term counselling is not merely a truncated form of counselling. In many instances it means a set number of sessions, although this number varies. While monetary constraints can and do limit the number of sessions, brief counselling cannot be defined merely in terms of time spent with clients, or in the number of sessions planned. It is an approach to counselling in its own right, focused on the solution or management of problems. Generally this means that the counsellor is more active, more challenging and more directive, and more willing to 'select' her clients, as brief therapy requires that the client be motivated towards solutions and capable of being focused on immediate positive change and outcome. The relationship so vital to the counselling process has little time to develop and to be fostered, but skilled counsellors may be able to establish the core conditions very rapidly. While the demand therefore is on the counsellor, as in long-term counselling, nevertheless the relationship depends to a greater extent on the client, whose willingness to participate and to trust so immediately are vital to the outcome.

Brief therapy is concerned with the identification rather than the exploration of problems or areas of concern or unhappiness, and focuses on the outcomes the client can identify as desirable.

Defining problems, setting goals and exploring ways of achieving these goals will differ between practitioners, but may include role-play, confrontation and 'homework', the setting of tasks linked to the work to provide a bridge between sessions. The ending of the work will include discussing strategies for coping in the future, and evaluation of the progress made in the sessions.

Focusing primarily on present difficulties, rather than on the client's past, the success of brief counselling is directly related to the ability of the client to identify and focus on her primary cause of concern and what she would like to do about it. The counsellor accepts this focus and works towards it with the client, finding ways of achieving this goal and evaluating the outcome. Short-term work depends on '...what is observable rather than on putative (supposed) causes'.[9] One of its most important elements is that clients are asked how they see their future, how they would like their lives to be. It is a 'future-focused' way of working, and it is never merely a curtailed version of open-ended counselling. It can be effective for certain types of difficulty, for certain clients in different circumstances, including voluntary or community services where there are long waiting lists, for employees who are in immediate work-stress situations, for students whose attendance will be dictated by term-time. The brief work may be an introduction to the nature and efficacy of counselling, and one result can be the seeking of more extensive work at a future date. It is important that the form and process of this approach remain the criteria for its use, rather than it being offered merely in terms of time and money available.

> ...counsellors need to be aware that there can be ethical problems with selecting the individual alone as the target of change, as this implies that the problem of stress resides primarily with the individual and, thus, that the onus to change lies on the individual.... Stress-

management interventions targeting individuals should only be carried out in the context of an appropriate response to stress.[10]

It is important that the role of management or the nature of the job be also considered in any attempt to reduce stress in the workplace.

There is no one model for 'short-term counselling', but rather a whole range of theories, ranging from renewable short-term contracts to intermittent brief therapy, which looks at psychological difficulties as being amenable to help in the same way as we bring our periodic colds and flu to our doctor. This suggests that we constantly repeat our patterns of distress and our attempts at solution, in the face of developmental changes and crises in our lives, and that access to a counsellor at these times of stress, for a brief exploration of the new problem area, would be sufficient to maintain our psychological health. There is the possibility that short-term counselling, with its duration decided on in advance, will have an element of quick-fix and diagnostic work, attempting and planning to change in a few sessions the ways of responding, relating and behaving, and the attitudes of a lifetime. The length of time needed depends on the difficulty or problem, and the vulnerable state of the client, and an estimate by the counsellor of what the client can tolerate. It also depends on the client's strengths before coming for help, the extent to which the client's trust has been previously damaged or betrayed, and the level of self-awareness and coping skills that the client possesses. The counsellor also tries to assess the client's motivation to change.

Where there is the expectation that the client will be able to clearly identify and pinpoint her 'problem', and where unhappiness without visible cause could pose difficulties, there is a danger that the counsellor could become impatient with a client who was confused and hesitant. In addition, if the identification of goals is the focus of much of the work, the possibility of the client seeing herself as a 'failure' increases. A client who has had unhappy educational experiences, for whom the word 'homework' conjures up the image of being 'stupid' and of being punished, could timidly retreat from the work too soon.

In general, the reason for offering brief counselling in both commercial and statutory sectors would often appear to be an economic one, with the accompanying danger that the needs of those paying the bills will take precedence over the needs of the consumer, the client. And Feltham points out that

> a major criticism of time-limited counselling is indeed that it may encourage a flight into spurious health and consequently represent a false economy.[11]

However, an awareness of the possible dangers and pitfalls, and the acknowledgement of the particular uses and benefits of short-term counselling where appropriate, make it difficult to agree totally with Brian Thorne:

> A new tyranny has been inaugurated in the name of an insatiable god whose... name is efficiency and his chief archangel is cost-effectiveness.[12]

Different methods of work are chosen or abandoned in terms of their success, and the difficulties of measuring 'success' in counselling makes for a shortage of clear-cut research on whether one form is more beneficial than others. Research continues, but in the main is not conclusive. 'Success cannot be measured unless there is a clear statement of original needs and goals....'[13] The possibility of such a clear statement of goals is unlikely when clients come for unspecified help. If at the end of our work, my client makes a statement of improved relationships, increased happiness and confidence, lessened fears and panics, then it is irrelevant whether I can claim it as *my* success or hers. She has succeeded in changing her life to a more positive state of being in the world, and it is this subjective statement and awareness that was my original aim. My client has identified where it hurt, and has achieved a measure of healing. The exploration and identification of the pain does not mean that it is excised, that it will vanish for ever. The triggers are still there, still potentially powerful, but her ability to cope with their impact has changed. She has grown through the pain, it will have become part of her like an old wound or scar, and it will no longer have the power to ambush her or devastate her in the way it once did. Whether she would achieve this without me, perhaps over a longer period of time, is a question to which there will never be an answer.

Ultimately, the form my counselling takes should depend on my efforts to meet the needs of my client. The theoretical background of the counsellor will determine her views of 'what is best for this client'. Once monetary considerations are introduced, then the decision is weighted, and not always by the client. '…the long-term therapist is unconsciously aware of the fiscal inconvenience of short-term work'.[14] This is a hard-hitting phrase, and one we cannot afford to ignore.

Often it is a crisis that precipitates the client into counselling, and when the crisis has passed, a review with the client can be valuable, to ascertain whether she wishes to explore further the topics thrown up by the crisis. Presenting problems are the lever that propels the client into counselling, and later on she may be in a better position to choose whether to continue on a path of self-discovery or end counselling at this stage. Mutual discussion and consultation can lead to an informed and empowered decision by the client, whether to stay or to go.

Feltham appeals for openness on the part of counsellors to remain aware of both the shortcomings and the benefits of different ways of working, and to be willing to at least allow the possibility of their efficacy. 'Limitations of time and money mean that the discoveries and methods of brief therapy and counselling must be experimented with and applied conscientiously'.[15] He further suggests that short-term counselling '…places an onus of accountability on therapists and counsellors',[16] but while this is patently true, there ought to be an equal onus on every conscientious counsellor, no matter what form of counselling she is working with. Perhaps it cannot be as acute for long-term counsellors, in the light of the longer time available for the work, but it certainly is there. Generally there does not appear to be agreement on a magic number of sessions, which will be of maximum benefit. Supporters and critics of both long- and short-term counselling flourish:

> Critics of brief (short-term) therapy say it cheats people of the opportunity to really explore themselves in depth; it is sometimes portrayed as an economic shortcut. Long-term therapy, however, is criticized as encouraging dependency and passivity, and discouraging problem-solving and therapeutic activity.[17]

Both are valid in their place, and both are open to abuse and to misuse. Provided that the counsellor remains aware of and open to the needs of each and every client, and willing to accept both the possibility of 'long term' being too comforting, and 'short term' being too sudden and sharp, then the question 'how long is a piece of string?' can be answered in the counselling world: 'As long as it takes to do the job required, depending on the client, on the counsellor, and on the circumstances'.

## Counselling Creatively

The method of counselling offered by a counsellor depends not only on her philosophical and theoretical training and beliefs, but also on her efforts to find a 'best fit' for her clients in general, and for each and every client in particular. Theories proliferate (the current figure suggested is about 300-400), some with a difference merely in terminology, some with a different method or duration or philosophical foundation, many quite similar but with differing emphasis on certain key ideas. With all these variations on the counselling theme, it is difficult to keep informed of what is available, but it is important that we as counsellors are willing to change, to improve the service we offer, or at least to question and re-choose the way we work.

Committed to venturing into the unknown with our clients, most counsellors are also willing to explore some of the ideas and theories of others, and the imaginative and creative possibilities these contain. In seeking ways of facilitating the client's exploration of self, a counsellor will look for alternatives to speech and words, where these do not appear sufficient or suitable for a particular client. A person who has difficulty recalling her childhood may find it useful to look at and describe herself in photographs, she may image each room in her house, or the garden, a favourite dress, a much loved pet. She could draw people or events important to her right now, or paint colours or shapes reflective of her feelings and moods. Often pain and fear are stored in our bodies, and clients may succeed in discharging stress and tension through movement.

A new approach is being fostered by Rogers' daughter Natalie, working in California as director of the Person-Centred Expressive Therapy Institute:

Movement, art, music, pottery, dream exploration and

writing all feature in this approach and clients who have grave difficulty in expressing themselves verbally find new possibilities for self-expression through essentially non-verbal channels.[18]

This is a welcome alternative to the 'talking therapies', which have been criticised as being of little benefit to those who are not very articulate, or who have had little experience of expressing their feelings and little vocabulary or facility in expressing them through words.

Whatever their theoretical training, counsellors have scope for creative ways of working with different mediums, as the relationship and the work appear to require it. It is of course essential that the counsellor be aware of the reasoning behind the new way of working, and the potential power in its application. A counsellor could seize on a popular image of counselling work, such as the Gestalt 'empty chair' or the idea of 'imaging' self, and introduce these powerful tools into the session, without at all being able to use the resulting shifts in the relationship or in the work. This could lead to reactions ranging from puzzlement to panic on the part of the client, and a sense of being adrift and helpless on the part of the counsellor.

One of the greatest assets in counselling is imagination, the ability to imagine the client's world as it is disclosed, what it is like to be this client, and also the imaginative use of resources to assist this difficult and often powerful disclosure.

The atmosphere and safe space within which the working alliance of client and counsellor can develop, '...can be described as an area between inner reality and the outer world, where fantasy and reality meet'.[19]

Obviously face-to-face language interaction is the most commonly used form of communication, with the client trying to put into words her feelings, thoughts and plans, and the counsellor responding with reflections, clarifications and accepting statements.

It often happens, however, that emotional states and memories are blocked by shame, embarrassment, lack of vocabulary, or are not present to the client's awareness. If, however, a client were to write down a painful episode in her life before a session, and then read it to the counsellor, she could somehow speak through the piece of paper, as if she were bouncing a signal from herself on to the paper and thence to the counsellor. The use of different mediums for indirect communication, such as dance, drama, drawing, can make it easier, more tolerable, to express some unhappy or painful event.

## Counselling as an Art

Colin Feltham draws attention to both the impromptu nature of much of the counsellor's work, and also to the use of 'artistic' methods of working:

> Many would concur with the view that counselling is primarily an interpersonal art or craft which draws from science and from many other disciplines too.[20]

The impromptu element is part of 'sitting with the uncertainty' discussed above, and working within that uncertainty. Clients sometimes express their conviction that the counsellor knows in advance the direction in which the work of a session will go and neatly guides it to a tidy conclusion just as the hour ends. It can be quite threatening for a client to become aware that the counsellor does not have a blueprint for the work or for the session, nor a plan for the 'successful' conclusion to the counselling relationship. The counsellor is working in the moment, and while she may see something of the outline of the client's world, and may postulate several potential outcomes, which of these paths the client will choose, or how she will find her way there, are not within the knowledge of the counsellor. For example, a client speaking of an unhappy situation at work may suggest that she leave that job, or she may attempt to change her position there, or seek to change the impact of the situation on her so that she can stay and survive. The counsellor's pledge is to remain with her while she explores the options, looks at the realities of her life at work and the pressures which may bind her to this particular job, and to support her in whatever she finally chooses to do. The areas of exploration will include the psychological make-up of the client, her experiences of life to date, how she has reacted to these and to those people connected with these experiences, her values and wishes for the future, her hopes and expectations.

The 'art and craft' element in each session consists of the skill of the counsellor in supplying opportunities through which the client may access her inner world, the ability to weave the strands supplied by the client into different patterns, and in having the imagination to enter into the world of the client and creatively offer opportunities for re-evaluation. This imaginative skill and sensitivity can be fostered by the counsellor being aware of the intricacies of her own life and the myriad of possibilities of her own exploration and outcome, and by her willingness to believe that the client has a similar complexity and variety of being.

> As a partner in the creation of a shared feeling-language, the therapist needs to be a kind of artist.[21]

The creative element lies in the selective focusing, highlighting and uncovering of significant elements in the client's exploration, threading our way through possibilities and potentials. New ways of working will be chosen by the counsellor to fit the client's circumstance, rather than merely to offer the counsellor an opportunity to 'try something new and different', and it is essential that the counsellor be aware both of the theoretical underpinning and the potential power and impact of the method. Equally it is essential that it is the client who remains the centre and the focus for the innovation, rather than the potential beauty and cleverness of the counsellor's interventions!

Feltham speaks of the 'aspired-to skill of finding and delivering the *mot juste*, the phrase, silence or gesture that may potently strike the right chords and deeply affect and benefit the client. ...The counsellor aspires, perhaps, to learn and refine the art or science of therapeutic response'.[22]

Awareness being a prerequisite for deliberate change, any technique or therapy that allows awareness into consciousness, or that pinpoints and releases hitherto hidden elements of the client's psychological world and her interaction with other people, can be usefully employed by the counsellor. There are many methods that attempt to shift the focus away from the talking therapies, each using a somewhat different method of accessing the client's hidden and relational worlds. I include here some brief examples of different ways of working, obviously excluding many of merit which have proved effective, and offering merely a picture postcard of others. These include drama therapy, art therapy, music therapy, sand therapy, narrative therapy, and a host of others.

> Creative expressions emerge from the unconscious rather than from 'ordinary' rationality. Examples of this are dreams, painting, drawing, sculpting, free association, visual imagery, ritual, improvised expressive movement and voice work. These activities reveal conscious and

unconscious wishes, fears, inner conflicts and hidden parts of the personality in symbolic form.[23]

### Psychodrama

Psychodrama is a method of group psychology that uses a dramatic format and theatrical terms.[24]

The basic premise is that the group will enact a brief spontaneous drama, with one member willing to allow her issues to be the central theme. The other group members play supporting roles and the facilitator/therapist is 'director'. The aim is to help the main actor (protagonist) to get in touch with feelings and emotions associated with the issue she has put forward for exploration, by opening her awareness through the channel of dramatic expression. When the drama ends, all the group members share their thoughts and feelings about the scene, and the protagonist will hopefully be more able to come to terms with past-life events, and find new ways of coping with the future. The work and the outcome of each and every piece of psychodrama is unique to that situation, and is a combination of inspiration and theoretical knowledge.

> Both artistry and method are needed to produce change.... Though the artistry of psychodrama has, as its foundation, solid technique, it is the element of taking a calculated risk that makes the work inspired rather than simply routine.[25]

This powerful method of working has been used to great effect with families, prisoners, sexually abused adults and adolescents, and indeed with many groups of people who have difficulty either expressing themselves verbally, or getting in contact with their earlier traumas. Precisely because of the power inherent in this method of working, it could be harmful if initiated by a counsellor without either training or experience in the area. Acting a part and becoming involved with other characters, feeling what it is like to be present in a specific way of thinking, feeling and behaving, being forced to draw on inner resources and memories to act this part, interacting with the roles being played by others, all contribute to discovery of hidden areas within the 'protagonist'. Her new awareness of different ways of looking at her own material leads to increased clarification through exploration, and to the changing of 'stuck' attitudes and ways of interacting with the 'real' world.

The use of drama as therapy enables the person to allow feelings and emotions, perhaps those that are seen as unacceptable to others or that are perceived as threatening to the person herself, to surface under another guise. Acting at a remove allows awareness of the process, and working with the therapist allows clarification, as well as admission to ownership of the role and of the emotional impact.

> '...the healing properties of Dramatherapy are contained in, and inseparable from, the dramatic process', and the theatre and drama are used '...to achieve psychological growth and change'.[26]

At the same time, the dramatherapist also shares in this inward view, as it is acted out in the playing of the characters, and can therefore be of help to the client in tentatively exploring, allowing and accepting the hidden facets of the client's inner troubled world.

### Art Therapy

The use of drawing and painting to express and explore our inner worlds offers another medium which bypasses the need to convey distress in words in order to share it. Hidden parts of the personality become visible in the client's drawings, and are illustrated graphically, and sometimes colourfully.

> Paintings, partly through the use of colour, are often vividly descriptive of a patient's mood, particularly as revealing an underlying depression which may not be manifest in the patient's talk or manner.[27]

Once these hidden parts are brought into the light of consciousness, they can be faced, examined, admitted, allowed. The resulting feelings of release and freedom, together with the acceptance by the therapist/counsellor of whatever material emerges, enable the client to recognise and accept complexities and events previously unknown.

Art therapy offers a channel through which the client can allow hidden material to become visible and 'named', other than through speech, and also offers visible images which can be discussed, explored and used as signposts towards the growth of the whole person.

### Music Therapy

Music is a powerful resonator through our past and through our memories, known and unknown. Hearing a piece of familiar music from long ago can re-create a time, a place, bodily sensations, echoed emotions.

> Music… can help in eliminating repressions and resistances and bring into the field of waking consciousness many drives, emotions and complexes which were creating difficulties in the unconscious.[28]

Use of musical instruments by a client can also afford a

method of communicating inner turmoil and forgotten feelings. It is the use of this channel by the client to access and express inner and often hidden or unconscious parts of herself and of her experience, which provides material for both client and counsellor to work with.

## Movement and Dance

Physical movement is a medium for self-expression, a basic part of communication, and a reflection of the feelings and emotions of the individual. The work of a dance and movement therapist is to encourage the client to become more free and therefore more expressive of her real self. She will also seek to remove barriers that both inhibit emotional release and maintain tensions and stress, and trigger memories of earlier events stored in the body and perhaps forgotten or hidden for a variety of reasons. In somewhat the same way, the use of massage can sometimes lower the defended barriers to emotional recollections, and link us, often with a suddenness that startles and overpowers us, with hidden memories and suppressed feelings, both good and bad.

## Sand Therapy

Sand therapy is another way of accessing hidden areas, a form of work that requires basic equipment (sand, a collection of potentially symbolic objects such as toy houses, animals, dolls).

The client, whether a child or an adult, chooses and positions these objects in the sandbox. The element of choice of objects, and the total lack of direction in this task by the counsellor, allows the client to link with and illustrate profound and hidden 'stories' in her life. There is an opportunity for the client, if she wishes, to speak about her created picture with the therapist, and highlight her new understanding or vision of the unfolded tale.

While uncomplicated, this is an extremely powerful process.

> Sometimes the best therapy is simply allowing the invisible to become visible.[29]

Sand therapy offers an alternative for those clients who are not articulate, whose very reason for coming for counselling may be their lack of speaking expertise. It also offers a method of working with those whose source of distress may be pre-verbal, or with clients whose experience is that of being rendered voiceless in their efforts to share or speak of their hurts and feelings, as a result of not being heard or listened to in previous attempts to ask for help or protection.

This form of therapy demands training and exploration on the part of the therapist. Used casually, it could be either empty or dangerous, since if 'the invisible becomes visible', the impact on the client can be greatly revealing and therefore potentially terrifying and destructive.

### Play Therapy

A different, but somewhat similar, form of counselling is play therapy, used primarily with children whose language or communication abilities are sparse, but whose inner worlds can be accessed through play material. The child recreates her experience and 'acts out' hostile and destructive feelings through the medium of dolls and toys. The counsellor, through observation and some verbal exchange, can see and understand what is beneath previously obscure and possibly violent behaviours.

### Narrative Therapy

Even in the 'talking therapies' there are different ways of looking at the medium.

>...the realisation that counselling and psychotherapy are based to some degree on the telling and sharing of stories is probably a feature in all orientations.[30]

In the telling of our story to someone who is prepared to listen in a warm and accepting manner, we can make sense of confusing experiences, share secrets that have burdened us for too long, release emotions, become aware that our experience is not uniquely 'strange', gain a wider perspective on the way we perceive the events, and experience a sense of completion and resolution. McLeod calls this 'narrative therapy', using our life stories to illuminate dark corners and secrets of the unconscious.

Work with clients can be seen as 'deconstructing' their life stories and their negative ways of looking at their personal histories, and through the counselling relationship 'reconstructing' these in the context of a broader perspective and a new way of seeing their lives.

>...it is important not to lose sight of the basic notion that people express themselves through stories, and that listening for, and to, the story is a powerful means of entering the world of the client.[31]

This 'narrative approach' is not simple, and like all techniques has inherent dangers if hastily or clumsily used. The narratives may be factual, but they carry strong emotional undercurrents, which need to be focused on and explored. Merely accepting the storied facts can be an over-simplification of basic truths, and can ignore the role of symbolism in our lives and in our self-awareness. Remaining aware that the story is the client's perception of events rather than any absolute factual truth is an important aspect of this narrative work.

Another way of tapping into our hidden selves, using writing as a therapeutic tool, is to keep a journal of our daily lives and thoughts and dreams. This helps us to face and confront fearful experiences, and lessens avoidance of these. It lifts painful material 'out of one's head' and externalises it on to paper, thereby making it possible to work through events, gradually absorbing them into our personal history, rather than allowing them to remain as ongoing stressful factors.

Obviously where clients have literacy difficulties, these will be taken into account, and the introduction of the idea of writing material will always be tentative.

Clients who have fears of being examined and of subsequently failing may approach any writing task very negatively, and this in itself can be a useful pointer towards an area for exploration.

### Dreams

Clients sometimes ask their counsellor to analyse or interpret a dream they have had, and it is tempting to do so. However, it is too easy to dissect a dream in terms that are relevant to ourselves, and to interpret symbolic representations in the dream as they would apply to us.

> ...the dream describes the inner situation of the dreamer, but the conscious mind denies its truth and reality, or admits it only grudgingly.[32]

Dreams can represent wishes, unexpressed and unconscious impulses, current anxieties, symbolic meanings, and innumerable other signs and portents reflected from the complexity of the client's personal world; they can appear entirely obvious in their meaning, or totally obscure. They can relate to a current event or a chance meeting of yesterday, or they can clearly picture a personal experience from childhood. More often they seem to evoke '...events of which the significance has not been fully appreciated by the dreamer'.[33]

Recurrent dreams or those with a recurrent theme can powerfully suggest an underlying feeling or emotion which can be directly focused on, since it arises from the inner unconscious world of the client. At times the counsellor is trying to guess at the emotional undertone of the client's story, perhaps hidden and defended, but with these dream memories, the accompanying emotions may be instantly clear, both to the client and to the counsellor, and can be explored more immediately. Dreams can be usefully related and re-experienced without precise interpretation of exactly what they mean.

> As a result, the telling of dreams and, perhaps even more, the listening to dreams is influenced by the fact that dreams can be used to discover information about the dreamer of which he himself, by reason or alienation, is unaware.[34]

If counselling is viewed, therefore, as the creative, imaginative and sensitive ability to accompany another on her exploration of painful, blocked memories and experiences, in order to facilitate change, then all these different forms of counselling and therapy have their place. Which form is chosen depends on the personality of the counsellor, on her theoretical training and experience, and on the background and presenting problems of her client population. The choice is also made by the client, who will often decide to see a particular counsellor because she works in one of these specific ways.

# REFERENCES

1. Kirschenbaum, H. and Henderson, V. Land (eds), *The Carl Rogers Reader* (London: Constable, 1990), p. 387.
2. Feltham, Colin, *What is Counselling?* (London: Sage, 1995), p. 150.
3. Rogers, Carl, *On Becoming a Person* (London: Constable, 1967/1990), pp. 11-12.
4. Shipton, Geraldine and Smith, Eileen, *Long-Term Counselling* (London: Sage, 1998), p. 155.
5. Ibid, p. 152.
6. Dryden, Windy and Feltham, Colin, *Counselling and Psychotherapy, A Consumer's Guide* (London: Sheldon Press, 1995), p. 103.
7. Shipton, Geraldine and Smith, Eileen, op. cit., p. 152.
8. Ibid., p. 113.
9. Feltham, Colin, *Time-Limited Counselling* (London: Sage, 1997), p. 36.
10. Cushway, Delia, 'New Directions in Stress' in *New Directions in Counselling*, Bayne, Rowan, Horton, Ian and Brimrose, Jenny (eds), (London: Routledge, 1996), p. 174.
11. Feltham, Colin, *Time-Limited Counselling*, op. cit., p. 11.
12. Thorne, Brian, 'Counselling and Psychotherapy: The Sickness and the Prognosis' in Palmer, Stephen and Varma, Ved (eds), *The Future of Counselling and Therapy* (London: Sage, 1997), pp. 153-66.
13. Dryden, Windy and Feltham, Colin, op. cit., p. 110.
14. Feltham, Colin, *Time-Limited Counselling*, op. cit., p. 20.
15. Feltham, Colin, *What is Counselling?* op. cit., p. 51.
16. Feltham, Colin, *Time-Limited Counselling*, op. cit., p. 22.
17. Dryden, Windy and Feltham, Colin, op. cit., p. 73.
18. Thorne, Brian, *Carl Rogers* (London: Sage, 1992/1995), p. 96.
19. Nolan, Inger, 'Imagery and Art as Symbolic Language in Psychotherapy' in *Éisteach*, vol. 1, no. 37, Summer 1996, Irish Association for Counselling and Therapy, p. 3.
20. Feltham, Colin, *What is Counselling*, op. cit., p. 16.
21. Hobson, Robert F., *Forms of Feeling – The Heart of Psychotherapy* (London: Tavistock, 1985), p. 91.
22. Feltham, Colin, *What is Counselling?* op. cit., pp. 157-8.
23. Nolan, Inger, op. cit., p. 2.
24. Holmes, Paul and Karp, Marcia (eds), *Psychodrama: Inspiration and Technique* (London: Tavistock/Routledge, 1991), p. 7.
25. Ibid., p. xvi.
26. Bracken, Angela, 'A Kitten, an Alien and Soft Stuff' in *Éisteach*, vol. 1, no. 37, Irish Association for Counselling and Therapy, p. 22.

27. Storr, Anthony, *The Art of Psychotherapy* (United Kingdom: Butterworth/Heinemann, 2nd edition, 1979/1990), p. 53.
28. Assagioli, Roberto, *Psychosynthesis* (United Kingdom: Aquarian Press, 1965/1990), p. 248.
29. Quinn-Berger, June, 'Sand Therapy, Communication, Explanation and Individuation' in *Éisteach*, vol. 1, no. 39, Winter 1996, Irish Association for Counselling and Therapy, p. 27.
30. McLeod, John, 'Working with Narratives' in *New Directions in Counselling*, Bayne, R., Horton, I., Bimrose, J. (eds), (London: Routledge, 1996), p. 189.
31. Ibid., pp. 197-8.
32. Jung, C. G., *Dreams* (London: Ark Paperbacks, 1985), p. 90.
33. Storr, Anthony, op. cit., p. 47.
34. Rycroft, Charles, *The Innocence of Dreams* (New Jersey, USA: Jason Aronson Inc., 1979/1996), p. 57.

# CHAPTER 9

## COUNSELLING AND OTHER MEDIUMS

*The politics of the client-centred approach is a conscious renunciation and avoidance by the therapist of all control over, or decision-making for, the client.*[1]

### Client Sources

A counsellor may base her work on a single theoretical model, but working with very differing clients in very differing settings may result in her changing her practical methods while staying within her chosen theoretical model. Certain aspects of the presenting story may call for specific changes in approach on the part of the counsellor. For example, the client coming from a court referral may have only six sessions within which to work, so the counsellor will try to adapt herself to this boundary, to work most effectively within it. If a client comes during the course of lengthy treatment for a potentially fatal disease, then the counsellor can be almost certain that all the work will proceed within the shadow of this illness, and be affected by it. Some of these different settings are looked at here.

### Counselling and Medicine

The way we view medicine is a reflection of our culture at any given time, and it is currently viewed as a science, as opposed to faith-healing or traditional herbal remedies. In a fairly short span, the swings of fashion in the treatment of 'mental' problems have moved from incarceration to physical interventions, to a sophisticated range of modern drugs and exploration of the physical activity of the brain. The advanced technology of scanning is highlighting the minute intricacies of the brain, but in an interesting reversal, is also emphasising other factors, psychological, environmental and social. For example, new findings which have located the brain cells that control our level of happiness, do not prove that if we could absorb quantities of a stimulative drug, then we would be happier people. Rather, they suggest that if we are involved in loving relationships, laugh a lot, think positively, then the brain cells involved will be stimulated and our 'happiness levels' will increase.

One of the greatest changes in the last ten years is the growing acceptance by doctors and psychiatrists of the potential benefit of counselling, and of the existence of counselling as a separate and beneficial resource. It is heartening to see collaboration beginning between doctors and counsellors/therapists, since such understanding and effective communication between these professions can only enhance the service each are giving to their clients/patients. A willingness to work together, and a recognition of the value of such team-work, focus on the well-being of the person coming for help, rather than on the old power struggles, where the validity of one approach in a particular circumstance somehow appeared to undermine the validity of a different or a side-by-side approach. It is an area where both disciplines need to listen to and respect the other, and where co-operation rather than competition is the goal.

The need to work with the whole person, whether ill or unhappy or socially ineffective, is comparatively new, but today sounds self-evident. It is no longer acceptable to talk about 'faulty brain wiring'. Instead, the structures of the person's life, his psychological state and his relational ability, all need to be acknowledged as having a part to play in all illness.

I marvel at how much is left unexplored regarding the *total* experience of patients and what disservice we do them if we do not acknowledge the entirety of their dilemma.[2]

This growing awareness on the part of doctors needs to be matched by counsellors, who at times can be quite opposed to the idea of medication to help a client. It is important that counsellors remain at least open to the idea of combining medication with counselling.

A client who becomes totally depressed, to the point where he cannot leave his house to keep appointments, needs something more than my accustomed way of working. If he were to receive some medication, he might reach a point of stability where he could begin again to take responsibility for his actions, and activate himself to seek psychological help through counselling. Perhaps he could then begin to explore possible triggers to his depression, possible strategies for recognising its onset and measuring its intensity and duration. Above all, he might realise that he is not alone, either in having this incapacitating condition, or in learning to live with it. Often the recognition that others use the same descriptive terms (it's like living in a glass jar; I'm looking out but cannot hear others or get in contact with them; I almost see it coming on, like a mist or cloud coming in the window) helps sufferers to accept that this is a periodic occurrence, and that it will pass. They can face the terror and acknowledge the isolation of depression once they look for help. The initial use of drugs may have brought this client to a stage where he is able to make a decision as to whether he wishes to choose the medical or the counselling option, or a combination of both. Co-operation between the doctor and the counsellor ensures that all aspects of the depression are attended to, including the possibility that depression can be a side-effect of some drugs used to treat physical illness.

There is a dividing line, often narrow and blurred, between illness and the inability to cope with life, between neurosis and psychosis. In neurosis, the person is failing to manage life experiences, and knows that he is so failing, aware that everything is 'getting on top of him' and that it is 'all too much for him'. In psychosis, the person is not aware of anything amiss. The voices heard, the role being played, is psychotic reality. It is the rest of the world that is out of kilter. The person has lost touch with reality, whereas for a neurotic person the world is all too real.

There is an ongoing debate as to the merits of counselling for people suffering from psychotic illness such as schizophrenia or manic depression. Carl Rogers argued that in most models of treatment for these conditions, the sufferer is dealt with as an *object* to be treated, whereas using the criteria of the Person-Centred Approach, he would be looked at as a *person*.[3]

He understood the medical model of treatment for schizophrenia as emphasising that this person has an illness to be eradicated, and that the psychotic material needs to be suppressed and eliminated. He was more interested in the possibility of the psychotic material being listened to as a 'chaotic but vital attempt at growth and self-healing', and understood as a potential indicator of where progress forward could occur.

There is a current suggestion that psychotic episodes have their basis in an 'actual inherent logic' which, given a combination of medication and counselling, could be tapped into and worked with. In contemporary society, short of time and perhaps threatened by the outward symptoms of the psychosis, we tend to 'medicate it away', but perhaps the echo of the idea will linger and be further explored in the future.

Another example of the co-operation between medicine and counselling is visible in the current thinking about the treatment for anorexia. This is now viewed on three levels, and while it is acknowledged that there is probably an underlying biological factor, emphasis is also placed firmly on the psychological element. It would appear that teenagers who are perfectionists and who have very low self-esteem are more at risk that their confident, easy-going counterparts. There is also thought to be a strong social element, since no one suffers from anorexia in countries where the image of beauty is not portrayed as essentially thin and skinny.

## Counselling and Nurses

Already bridging the divide between medicine and counselling are those in the nursing profession, who are ideally placed within the medical world, with intimate and personal contact with patients and a knowledge of the medical implications of those in their care. The last number of years has seen in medicine the beginning of a shift from a 'medical model' to an interpersonal relationship model, and hopefully this will facilitate the recognition of nurses' role and the value of listening and responding to the patient on a more human level.

> Recent literature suggests that nurses now view counselling as an integral aspect of their role.[4]

The role of nurses in the medical scene is focused more on healing than on disease or medical intervention, and they can therefore see beyond these to the whole person: how they manage their pain, what their worries are about family, how afraid they are of what happens next. Perceived as more accessible, they spend more time with their patients as they carry out their duties. Power can be seen to reside in doctors: power to give or withhold medicines and painkillers, to decide whether or not to operate, to discharge or to keep in hospital.

Equality is more possible with nurses, and they are seen as more likely to listen to our stories.

Nurses were using counselling skills even before the term was coined: listening, attending, reading beyond the words said, aware of patients as 'real' people beneath their presenting symptoms. More and more nurses are leaving work on the wards to train as counsellors. In an increasingly technical world, it is easy to lose the person to descriptions like 'the man in bed number four', or 'the hysterectomy in ward one', and aware of this tendency, nurses are drawing back from the 'instrumentation' to concentrate on the whole person, in a counselling capacity. Many hospitals too are more aware of the need to focus on the patient as person, as part of a social system, of a family. Relatives throng the corridors of hospitals, frightened by the illness, but also bemused by the building, the apparent impersonality of it all, by the feeling of being merely a number amongst numbers. Nurse counsellors can work with all members of this wide circle, supplying not only counselling skills (and where necessary, more in-depth counselling), but also knowledge, and therefore clarity, concerning many of the medical mysteries and the questions posed by both patient and relatives.

## Psychosomatic Symptoms and Stress

There is increasing awareness of the effects of stress and its attendant demons, which can play a large part in physical illness such as ulcers, asthma, headache, back pain.

Where disease or damage cannot be pinpointed, and where x-rays show no obvious source for pain, then psychological factors will be looked at. These can either be the direct cause of the symptoms, or they can accompany an obvious physical illness. The lack of an explanation for the physical pain and distress can exacerbate the suffering, because in the absence of a label, the person can luridly imagine all manner of disease, and the level of stress and tension increases even more. The use of the term 'psychosomatic' can in itself cause distress, as sufferers imagine that the doctor is saying in effect: 'It's all in your mind, you're imagining the pain'.

Of course the distinction between physical and psychological causes for illness are ill-defined, and not in any way clear-cut. For example, a person with MS may become so depressed and defeated at the future outlook, that the illness strikes more seriously, because the immune system is not functioning at its best due to the hopelessness of the patient. It does appear that a positive frame of mind can lessen the impact of an illness or disease, and at times can even go some way towards lessening the physical symptoms. However, to claim that mind can triumph over matter to such an extent that all illness is caused by our own negativity is both implausible and cruel. The implication is: 'She's very ill and if she could think positively, she could become well, therefore it's her own fault. She's just not trying hard enough to be positive, or not doing it right'. The burden of guilt this places on a sick person can become in itself a cause of deterioration.

Clients presenting from a medical referral may therefore be afraid (of what might be the matter), angry (at being referred to a 'shrink'), confused (about a physical pain appearing to be diagnosed as 'mental'), frustrated (because there doesn't appear to be a bottle or a pill to take). Added to the usual range of feelings which accompany a client into a first appointment, may be a deep suspicion that they are not being told everything, that they are being 'fobbed off', and the counsellor may have a difficult task establishing the beginnings of trust in the relationship. The frustration of some doctors with their patients who seem either not to be ill at all, or not to respond to accepted remedies, can be heard in phrases such as 'the worried well', 'heart-sink patients', which reflect a negative reaction to intransigent symptoms apparently outside medical expertise.

Depression and anxiety are common causes of somatic symptoms, depression causing exhaustion, loss of sleep and appetite as well as hopeless misery, and anxiety producing chest pains, free-floating fear, and dizziness, breathlessness, faintness or panic attacks.

The experience of loss and trauma may precede the onset of depression, and the decision as to whether to treat the physical symptoms, the psychological or both together, is a difficult one for the doctor or the counsellor, whichever sees the person first. This confusion can lead '...to uncertainty in both client and counsellor about when it is appropriate to offer psychological help and when to support the client in the search for a medical answer'.[5] There is no easy solution to this dilemma. It is yet another uncertainty to sit with.

Counselling with clients who present with psychosomatic symptoms obviously begins with an acceptance of the client's description of these symptoms as real, and encouraging him to look for links and connections to events, examining the background, and trying to identify the feeling-tone connected with the symptoms. Understanding the underlying causes for such symptoms can often be a major step towards at least lessening them. In a simple example, tension and fear can lead to constriction of blood vessels leading to a headache, and relaxation exercises can lessen the pain. The client can then concentrate on exploring the causes of the tension.

Another example is when a client may unconsciously be finding her need for attention, for company, met when she is ill, when pain results in hospitalisation. Such pain may be particularly amenable to alleviation if a connection is made with her need for affection. An understanding of 'why' may be reached through rediscovery of a neglected childhood, when attention and love were experienced only at times of illness, and the client may find, as a result, new ways of achieving companionship. The unconscious attempt to recreate and retrieve happier circumstances is very strong.

Medication can be important in some forms of psychological distress, such as chronic insomnia or severely high levels of anxiety and panic attacks. Not everyone might agree with Michael Corry that '...medication is an adjunct to psychotherapy and used judiciously can have marvellous effects', fearful that it is but a short step to medication being used as a focus solely on the symptom rather than on the cause. But Corry goes on to say that if a doctor works solely with the physiological, chemical approach, then '...the cognitive and emotional chaos just continues'.[6]

The inclusion of counselling skills training within medicine, along with an acknowledgment of the need to explore the impact of the work on the person of the doctor, has opened up new avenues for many doctors. It is helping to highlight the similarities in the approaches, rather than merely concentrating on the differences, and this interaction is leading to learning on both sides.

> ...an ethical commitment to, and respect for, patients, combined with an ability to engage in self awareness, should be integral to what makes a good doctor.[7]

This acknowledgement that self-awareness is important for the well-being of both doctor and patient, making the doctor's work more effective, and affording some protection for the well-being of the doctor herself, is an important step in the relationship between medicine and counselling. Through increased self-awareness, leading to empathy and understanding of the whole person, a greater tolerance of uncertainty will be found. Eoin Hegarty suggests that general practice is the branch of medicine which contains the least certainty, and that 'research has shown that the most successful GP will be the one who can manage that uncertainty as opposed to one who diagnoses'.[8]

Being comfortable with uncertainties, whether as doctor or as counsellor, enables me to remain open to possibilities and alternative avenues of procedure, and to a climate of respect and trust between me and my client/patient, resulting in more effective co-operation and identification of the shared goal. 'Patient autonomy' is a term that is becoming more widely used, indicating the ability – and also the *right* – of patients to think and act independently, to make decisions about their illness and to share these with their doctor. This in turn imposes a duty on doctors to empower their patients to decide for themselves what mode of treatment they would choose, if there is a choice to offer. The role of counsellor in medical settings links with this: '…counselling offers clients an opportunity to relinquish their passive patient roles and engage in a relationship which in itself promotes change and healing'.[9] In effect, the client/patient is enlisted to work positively on his own behalf.

Many general medical practices today have a counsellor working in close contact with the doctor concerned, allowing for ease of referral and consultation concerning the person who has come looking for help. Counselling in these settings may have a preponderance of clients focused firmly on illness, loss, death and dying, whether the person is directly involved or at a remove, such as the family and relatives of the sick person. In the counselling sessions, the illness can appear to occupy a third seat, pervading and haunting the work, so that the counsellor has difficulty in seeing the person involved, rather than a 'person who is ill'. Similarly, a counsellor could find it distracting to work with a client who has a handicap, not because she has difficulty or embarrassment about a disability, but because she may find it hard to challenge in any way a person who is already struggling with illness or with disability. The protective tendency, present in us all, may be harder to dislodge in such situations. Illness can also trap the client in a place where all happenings are flagged as 'after I heard' or 'before I was diagnosed', and he can lose sight of himself as a presence, a real self, irrespective of illness or health. In the opposite way, sometimes the counsellor can talk with a sick client and his family without hearing any mention of illness, as if by not drawing attention to it, the illness would disappear. (This has been likened to the 'elephant in the kitchen' scenario, where a family lives with an elephant in the middle of their home, without ever referring to its existence. Life is carried on around the animal, accommodations are made to avoid the space he takes up, and he looms at all times above the assembled family. But he is ignored, never mentioned, and life continues as if he were never there!) At times a family comes for help in the hope that the counsellor will openly refer to the fact that this person is ill, very ill, and it needs to be discussed.

A further benefit of introducing counselling in a medical setting is well expressed by Patricia East: 'When all medical treatments have been exhausted, counselling and psychotherapy cannot alter what is happening but they can offer the possibility of transforming the experience'.[10]

For many years, counsellors have struggled to have more contact with doctors, on equal footing, looking for recognition of the value of counselling for some patients. As this would appear now to be becoming more of a reality, with more doctors acknowledging a place for counselling, and trainee doctors being more exposed to the practical application of counselling techniques and theories, perhaps it is also time for counsellors to have a greater sense of the role of medicine in treating the whole person.

> I'd like to think… that counsellors had a sense of where general practitioners are coming from, or the type of issues that are presented in the GP's practice, and the highly skilled way the GP responds…. There needs to be a development of their (counsellors') sense of when medication is appropriate, and for them to work in harmony with that.[11]

This is a timely response to counsellors' requests for more awareness on the part of doctors of the benefits of counselling, turning the tables to suggest that counsellors would do well to have a better understanding of general practice and all medical practice.

### Reluctant and Resistant Clients

In other settings, reluctant clients can create a whole new set of difficulties for the counsellor and the counselling process. Generally counselling can only achieve results if the client is willing to work positively, if painfully, towards change. But counsellors often find themselves trying to work with clients who have no wish to be present, resent the whole experience of being 'sent' for counselling, and refuse totally to co-operate in any way with the process. In schools, the guidance counsellor can at times be viewed as a last option for unruly students! More and more, the law courts are including six or so counselling sessions as part of probation requirements, and employees are being encouraged to 'see someone' about their difficulties or poor work practices. Sometimes silent and surly and truculent, such clients can test a counsellor's patience, and even more, both her belief in the whole process of counselling and in her own ability as a communicator. People who are resentfully 'putting in their time' will not work effectively with the counsellor.

The resistance of the client needs to be acknowledged, aired and explored, with the emphasis on the client's choice about outcomes, even though they do not have a choice about being physically present. Entering into argument or persuasion will merely heighten and strengthen resistance to co-operation or change of any kind. Focusing on what the person chooses to do in the moment, and then working to clarify the consequences of their decisions, will help this client to make informed decisions and to take responsibility for these.

Too often the counsellor is seen as yet another establishment figure, bent on imposing discipline, order and 'right' thinking on this person. If this image can be changed, and a more positive aspect can be shown, then some work may be done. But the new image obviously must be a genuine and a congruent one, springing from the heart and mind of the counsellor, or it will be seen for what it is, a tepid attempt to be 'nice', and the potential client will be even more entrenched in his isolation. It is possible to explain what counselling is, what it is not, and my unwillingness to force it on anyone. In response to a statement of non-cooperation, I might answer: 'We have an hour. How would you like to use it? We can sit in silence, or we can discuss any issue you like. You might like to know more about my work'. The hope here is that, by forging even a thread of relationship, some kind of trust can begin, and some kind of work can follow. A familiar pitfall is to say to the client: it is your time, what do you want to discuss?, and then, fearful or uneasy with the silence, the counsellor proceeds to fill it herself, and talk busily 'at' the other person. If I offer an hour of time to another person, and say it is yours to fill, then it is important that I do not immediately take it back, claim it for myself, and proceed to fill it with my own concerns, or worse still, admonishments and platitudes about living a better life!

Perhaps the most important issue here is that the counsellor does not become involved in a conflict situation, responding as opponent in the game the client is locked into. An aggressive statement does not have to call up an aggressive response from the counsellor. Declining to respond in the way this person is accustomed to can shift the pattern and rearrange the expected dynamic in this relationship. Often the most telling aspect, for the client, at the beginning of this relationship, is that here is someone who does not respond in the socially normal way. The counsellor steadfastly remains her own self, and this can be a totally new experience for an aggressive or an angry client. Accustomed to being met with returned aggression or a defensive response, the client can be forced to change his own response in return, and a relationship of sorts can begin. I remember a difficult ten minutes sitting with a potential client in a prison. She was chewing what I thought was gum, but quickly realised was an open safety pin. It took all my willpower not to tell her to stop, that she would die if she swallowed it, and all the other motherly strictures that demanded utterance. Finding I wasn't going to react, she lost interest in the pin after a few minutes, took it out, and we subsequently worked quite well. My determination to afford her responsibility and decision-making for herself, particularly in a setting where she was free in no other way, aroused her curiosity, to the point where she wanted to at least begin this different relationship.

The contract and the boundaries between a reluctant client and the counsellor must be crystal clear, and must deal with the reality of confidentiality (will a report be required by the referring person or body, and if so, will the client see it before it is presented), length of contract, who is paying, has the client any choice about attendance? Openness and the 'transparency' advocated by Rogers, are essential in all counselling contracts, but even more vital in this fraught relationship between counsellor and reluctant client.

In an article by Mairéad Kavanagh, she outlined the guidelines she uses effectively in her own work:

> One process which works well is using a three-way meeting between client, counsellor and probation officer and in this meeting some of the contract is explored and set out with the agreement of all three present. Usually confidentiality is discussed and the limits and boundaries to this are set. These are that client confidentiality stands and will be broken only if there is a serious threat to the health, life or well-being of the client or another person.[12]

This clear statement not only sets the boundaries with the agreement of the client, but it also allows the client to be aware that she has personal control. The counsellor is willing to help if the client wishes to be helped. No coercion will be looked for or used, other than perhaps the physical attendance of the client at the set times laid down by the referring agency. '...in the beginning, middle and end the client chooses or determines what happens...'.[13]

Reluctance or resistance is also encountered where a client looks at options for exploration, and decides she is not willing to face these painful areas which have been highlighted. She looks at the hurt, and draws back, and while this is of course the client exercising her choice of direction, it is important that the counsellor be aware of this choice, and illuminate it for the client, so that she too is aware of what is happening.

> An avoidance action, a 'defence', always says something about what is being defended. That statement is crucial in psychotherapy.[14]

This conflict between stability, staying with the 'devil you know', and change, where something different and unknown is tried, is a fearful place for a client. In the majority of cases, the risk is taken to explore the change, but sometimes the fear is greater, and the client withdraws and tries to clutch at the old certainties. If the choice is to avoid a new direction, and the options are weighed and discussed, then it can be an informed choice. Too often, however, the avoidance is unconscious and unmentioned, and if the counsellor also avoids this area, then it could remain a hidden minefield in the client's future. If the counsellor successfully highlights and vocalises the client's reluctance or refusal to explore this area, then it is possible that the client will discover where the avoidance reaction springs from. Even if the client still refuses or declines to explore the difficulty, the fact of avoidance is known and spoken, and while accepting the client's decision, the counsellor has pinpointed a topic that may be explored in the future, in the safety of the counselling relationship.

For some clients, a state of constant resistance is more difficult to clarify, as it is a pervasive aspect of their lives. Their stated belief is that it is *others* who need to change, and that these same *others* are determined to do them down, and that life in general is against them. This unwillingness or inability to take responsibility for any part of their unhappiness or misfortune renders them helpless in the face of an unkind fate, and they see no point in trying to change or become responsible for their actions or reactions.

If they do present for counselling, the task of the counsellor would be to encourage ownership of their feelings, thoughts and actions, and to highlight their chosen role as victims, along with the possibility of becoming empowered through exploration and change. If this were presented abrasively, the counsellor would merely be classed along with all other 'oppressors', and the feelings of victimisation would be strengthened. If the counsellor can find words which the client is able and willing to hear, then the message might be simply: 'You are not responsible for the roadblocks that life throws in your way. You are only responsible for your attitudes, actions and reactions…. Nobody is entitled to take your self-responsibility away. However, you can give it away'.[15] Offering this choice places the responsibility for engaging in the counselling work firmly on the client, and offers a way of empowering him to take similar responsibility for himself, his life, his decisions. In the final analysis, the counsellor may be willing to work with the client, but the client has the choice of whether or not to engage.

Obviously a good counselling relationship is not possible with *everyone* who comes for counselling. There are two people in the relationship: a client who may be quite unwilling to meet me on any level, and myself, who may not be able to bridge this divide, who may find it too difficult to be positive towards a particular person who is sullen or angry or jealous, or physically frightening. I do find that if I can manage to meet, or even to glimpse, a fearful vulnerable inner person behind the anti-social façade, then it is possible for me to be present to this person, offering them the possibility of a relationship. The choice is then theirs as to whether we can work together, or at least form some minimal pact from which to begin.

## Limitations

Like any emerging profession, counselling has its limitations and its critics, but it is also constantly growing and improving, since to become a static would be to stagnate. As a non-statutory profession, counselling does not have the power to regulate and control the practices of all who call themselves counsellors and therapists, in either the United Kingdom or Ireland.

Currently in the UK anyone without fear of prosecution may call himself or herself a counsellor or psychotherapist.[16]

Both the Irish Association for Counselling and Therapy (IACT) and the British Association for Counselling (BAC) have a Code of Ethics and Practice, and a system of accreditation, both of individuals and of counselling training courses, but their rules and standards are not binding on non-members. These systems of accreditation are designed to protect clients and counsellors, to educate the public, and to raise standards of training and practice. In both countries, this accredited membership is becoming a requirement for applicants for counselling positions.

It would be foolish to believe counselling is a panacea for all human ills – spiritual, physical or psychological. It is sometimes suggested that where any counselling theory or practice proves ineffective, then this is a reflection merely of the lack of expertise of the counsellor, rather than a failure of either counselling or the relevant theory.

> Deterioration in psychotherapy is usually the result of either poor selection of patients or bad therapeutic practice. Not all patients are appropriate subjects for psychotherapy, or for a particular type of therapy.[17]

The use of the core conditions of Rogers in any relationship, with individuals or with groups, renders the counsellor open and loving and accepting. Whether or not the resulting relationship is a counselling one depends on the circumstances and the willingness or ability of the other person to respond and to engage.

In all areas and branches of counselling and psychotherapy, there is a paucity of research into the effectiveness and the outcomes of counselling, and while this is somewhat understandable due to the nature of the work and the difficulty of expressing the results of any human interactions in scientific terms, it is nevertheless a gap which the profession needs to find ways of closing. At this particular time, critics of counselling are also suffering from a lack of hard evidence to support their criticisms, and can find themselves writing of personal or anecdotal evidence, or else asking somewhat querulous questions to which there is no answer. The most effective of these encourage the profession to ask questions of themselves and their work, and to take nothing for granted, not even the foundations of their chosen theories.

## Positive Outcomes

Counselling today has a confident and broadly-based professional outlook, grown far beyond the limited dreams of the early days of the IACT and BAC. However, the basic aim of counselling has not changed: to help troubled people '...to move away from a state of psychological maladjustment or disturbance towards a state of psychological adjustment',[18] to become the 'fully functioning person' described by Carl Rogers,[19] able to trust himself rather than look to others for approval, not afraid to take responsibility for his own actions and decisions, free to think and to act as he judges best. How this movement towards psychological adjustment is achieved, theoretically and practically, depends on the willingness of the client to be open to the experience, and on the training, personality and present equilibrium of the counsellor. It is an important and demanding enterprise we are engaged in. Much of the work is intangible, of the moment, yet the results can be real and lasting. The counselling world may be one of uncertainty, of contradictions, of risk, but above all it is full of transformations and hope.

#### REFERENCES

1. Kirschenbaum, H. and Henderson, V. Land (eds), *The Carl Rogers Reader* (London: Constable, 1990), p. 381.
2. Tubridy, Áine, 'Medical and Counselling Issues in a Mind-Body Practice' in *Éisteach*, vol. 2, no. 5, Summer 1998, Irish Association for Counselling and Therapy, p. 3.
3. Kirschenbaum, H. and Henderson, V. Land (eds), op. cit., p. 389.
4. Boland, Margaret, 'The Counselling Role of the Nurse in a General Setting' in *Éisteach*, vol. 2, no. 5, op. cit., p. 38.
5. Sanders, Diana, *Counselling for Psychosomatic Problems* (London: Sage, 1996), p. 12.
6. Corry, Michael, 'Getting the Balance', interview with Carl Berkeley in *Éisteach*, vol. 2, no. 5, op. cit., p. 22.
7. O'Carroll, Austin, 'Appreciating Difference' in *Éisteach*, vol. 2, no. 5, op. cit., p. 25.
8. Hegarty, Eoin, 'A Therapeutic Subversive at Work Within Medical Practice', interview with Sheila Killoran-Gannon, in *Éisteach*, vol. 2, no. 5, op. cit., p. 36.
9. East, Patricia, *Counselling in Medical Settings* (England: Open University Press, 1995), p. 86.
10. Ibid., p. 105.
11. Clune, Brendan, 'A Doctor Refers' in *Éisteach*, vol. 2, no. 5, op. cit., p. 14.
12. Kavanagh, Mairéad, 'The Non-Voluntary Client' in Eisteach, vol. 2, no. 2, Autumn 1997, op. cit., p. 20.
13. Ibid., op. cit., p. 23.
14. Hobson, Robert F., *Forms of Feeling, The Heart of Psychotherapy* (London: Tavistock, 1985), p. 239.
15. Reville, William, 'Science Today', *The Irish Times*, 26 October 1998.
16. Feltham, Colin, *What is Counselling?* (London: Sage, 1995), p. 44.
17. Holmes, Jeremy and Lindley, Richard, *The Values of Psychotherapy* (England: Oxford University Press, 1989), p. 36.
18. Thorne, Brian, *Carl Rogers* (London: Sage, 1992), p. 35.
19. Kirschenbaum, H. and Henderson, V. Land (eds), op. cit., p. 250.

# APPENDIX

*In 1965, Carl Rogers participated in making a film, using a half-hour session with a client, Gloria, to illustrate his theory in practice. (Albert Ellis and Fritz Perls also participated in the making of this film, also working with Gloria for thirty minutes.) In his introduction, Rogers briefly outlined what he hoped to achieve with his client, and how he would proceed. This gives a concise outline of the core conditions, and is reproduced here in full.*

'From my own years of therapeutic experience, I have come to feel that if I can create the proper climate, the proper relationship, the proper conditions, a process of therapeutic movement will almost inevitably occur in my client. You might ask: what is this climate? What are these conditions? Will they exist in the interview with the woman I am about to talk with, whom I have never seen before? Let me try to describe very briefly what these conditions are, as I see them.

First of all, one question is: Can I be real in the relationship? This has come to have an increasing amount of importance to me over the years. I feel that genuineness is another way of describing the quality I would like to have. I like the term congruence, by which I mean that what I am experiencing inside is present in my awareness and comes out through my communication. In a sense, when I have this quality I'm all in one piece in the relationship. There's another word that describes it for me – I feel that in the relationship I would like to have a transparency. I would be quite willing for my client to see all the way through me, so that there would be nothing hidden. And when I am real in this fashion that I am trying to describe, then I know that my own feelings will often bubble up into awareness and be expressed, but be expressed in ways that won't impose themselves on my client.

Then the second question I would have is: Will I find myself prizing this person, caring for this person? I certainly don't want to pretend a caring that I don't feel. In fact, if I dislike my client persistently, I feel it's better that I should express it. But I know that the process of therapy is much more likely to occur, and constructive change is much more likely, if I feel a real spontaneous prizing of this individual with whom I am working, a prizing of this person as a separate individual. You can call that quality acceptance, you can call it caring, you can call it a non-possessive love if you wish. I think any of these terms tend to describe it. I know that the relationship will prove more constructive if it's present.

Then the third quality: Will I be able to understand the inner world of this individual, from the inside? Will I be able to see it through her eyes? Will I be able to be sufficiently sensitive to move around inside the world of her feelings, so that I know what it feels like to be *her*, so that I can sense not only the surface meanings but some of the meanings that lie somewhat underneath the surface. I know that if I can let myself sensitively and accurately enter into her world of experience, then change and therapeutic movement are much more likely.

Well, suppose I am fortunate and that I do experience some of these attitudes in the relationship, what then? Well, then a variety of things are likely to happen. Both from my clinical experience, and from our research investigations, we find that if attitudes of the sort that I have described are present, then quite a number of things will happen.

She will explore some of her feelings and attitudes more deeply. She is likely to discover some hidden aspects of herself that she wasn't aware of previously. Feeling herself prized by me, it's quite possible she'll come to prize herself more. Feeling that some of her meanings are understood by me, then she can more readily perhaps listen to herself, listen to what is going on within her own experience, listen to some of the meanings she hasn't been able to catch before. Perhaps if she senses a realness in me, she'll be able to be a little more real within herself.

I suspect there will be a change in the manner of her expression, at least this has been my experience in other instances. From being rather remote from her experiencing, remote from what's going on within her, it's possible that she'll move toward more immediacy of experiencing, that she will be able to sense and express what is going on in her in the immediate moment. From being disapproving of herself, it is quite possible she will move toward a greater degree of acceptance of herself. From somewhat of a fear of relating, she may move toward being able to relate more directly and to encounter me more directly. From construing life in somewhat rigid black and white patterns, she may move toward more tentative ways of construing her experience, and of seeing the meanings in it. From a locus of evaluation which is outside of herself, it is quite possible she will move toward recognising a greater capacity within herself for making judgements and drawing conclusions.

So those are some of the changes that we have tended to find and I think that they are all changes that are characteristic of the process of therapy or therapeutic movement. If I have any success in creating the kind of conditions that I have described initially, then we may be able to see some of these changes in this client, even though I know in advance that our contact is going to be very brief.'[1]

---

1. Psychological and Educational Films, *Three Approaches to Psychotherapy, Part 1 – Carl Rogers*, Everett L. Shostrom, Producer, 1965. Used with permission.

# BIBLIOGRAPHY

Assagioli, Roberto, *Psychosynthesis* (United Kingdom: Crucible, Aquarian Press, 1965/1990).

Barkham, M., 'Exploratory Therapy in Two-Plus-One Sessions' in *British Journal of Psychotherapy* 6 (1), 1989.
Bass, Ellen and Davis, Laura, *The Courage to Heal* (New York: Harper and Row, 1988).
Bayne, R., Horton, I., Bimrose, J. (eds.), *New Directions in Counselling* (London: Routledge, 1996).
Berman, Linda, *Beyond the Smile: The Therapeutic Use of the Photograph* (London: Routledge, 1993).
Boland, Margaret, 'The Counselling Role of the Nurse in a General Setting' in *Éisteach*, vol. 2, no. 5, Irish Association for Counselling and Therapy.
Boyne, Edward (ed.), *Psychotherapy in Ireland* (Dublin: The Columba Press, 1993).
Bracken, Angela, 'A Kitten, an Alien and Soft Stuff' in *Éisteach*, vol. 1, no. 37, Summer 1996, Irish Association for Counselling and Therapy.
Brazier, David (ed.), *Beyond Carl Rogers* (London: Constable, 1993).
Brazier, David, 'The Necessary Condition is Love' in Brazier, David (ed.), *Beyond Carl Rogers* (London: Constable, 1993).
Brazier, David, *Zen Therapy* (London: Constable, 1995).
Browne, Ivor, *Sunday Business Post*, Dublin, 11 July 1999, p. 17.

Carey, Gerald, *Theory and Practice of Counselling and Psychotherapy*.
Casement, Patrick, *On Learning from the Patient* (London: Routledge/Tavistock, 1985/1992); *Further Learning from the Patient* (London: Routledge/Tavistock, 1990).

Clune, Brendan, 'A Doctor Refers' in *Éisteach*, vol. 2, no. 5, Irish Association for Counselling and Therapy.

Corney, Roslyn (ed.), *Developing Communication and Counselling Skills in Medicine* (London: Tavistock/Routledge, 1991).

Corry, Michael, 'Getting the Balance', interview with Carl Berkeley, in *Éisteach*, vol. 2, 5, Summer 1998, Irish Association for Counselling and Therapy.

Culley, Sue and Wright, James, 'Brief and Time-Limited Counselling' in Palmer, Stephen and McMahon, Gladeana (eds.), *Handbook of Counselling* (London: Routledge, in association with British Association for Counselling, 1997).

Cushway, Delia, 'New Directions in Stress' in Bayne, R., Horton, I., Bimrose, J. (eds.), *New Directions in Counselling* (London: Routledge, 1996).

Denman, C., 'Questions to be Answered in the Evaluation of Long-Term Therapy' in Aveline, M. and Shapiro, D. A. (eds.), *Research Foundations for Psychotherapy Practice* (Chichester: John Wiley/Mental Health Foundation, 1995).

Dryden, W., *'It Depends': A Dialogue with Arnold Lazarus* (United Kingdom: Open University Press, 1991); *Therapists' Dilemmas* (London: Harper and Row, 1985).

Dryden, W. (series ed.), *Counselling in Action* series (London: Sage, 1991); *Developing Counselling* series (London: Sage, 1994).

Dryden, W., Charles-Edwards, D., Woolfe, R. (eds.), *Handbook of Counselling in Britain* (England: Routledge, in association with British Association for Counselling, 1989/1994).

Dryden, W. and Feltham, C., *Brief Counselling: Practical Guide for Beginning Practitioners* (United Kingdom: Open University Press, 1992); *Counselling and Psychotherapy, A Consumer's Guide* (Sheldon Press, 1995).

East, Patricia, *Counselling in Medical Settings* (England: Open University Press, 1995).

Edwards, David, 'Supervision Today: The Psychoanalytic Legacy' in Shipton, Geraldine (ed.), *Supervision of Psychotherapy and Counselling* (UK: Open University Press, 1997).

*Éisteach:* Journal of the Irish Association for Counselling and Therapy, Dublin, Ireland.

Elton Wilson J., *Time-Conscious Psychological Therapy* (London: Routledge, 1996).

Feltham, Colin, *Time-Limited Counselling* (London: Sage, 1997).

Feltham, Colin, *What is Counselling?* (London: Sage, 1995).

Feltham, Colin and Dryden, Windy, *Developing Counsellor Supervision* (London: Sage, 1994), p. x.

Frankl, Viktor E., *Man's Search for Meaning* (New York: Pocket Books, 1963).

Giovacchini, Peter L., *Borderline Patients, the Psychosomatic Focus and the Therapeutic Process* (USA: Jason Aronson Inc., 1993).

Hawkins, P. and Shohet, R., *Supervision in the Helping Professions* (United Kingdom: Open University Press, 1989).

Hegarty, Eoin, 'A Therapeutic Subversive at Work Within Medical Practice', interview with Sheila Killoran-Gannon, in *Éisteach*, vol. 2, no. 5, Irish Association for Counselling and Therapy.

Hobson, Robert F., *Forms of Feeling, The Heart of Psychotherapy* (London: Tavistock, 1985).

Holmes, J. and Lindley, R., *The Values of Psychotherapy* (Oxford: Oxford University Press, 1989/1990).

Holmes, Paul and Karp, Marcia (eds.), *Psychodrama: Inspiration*

*and Technique* (London: Tavistock/Routledge, 1991), p. 7.
Howe, David, *On Being a Client* (London: Sage, 1993).

Inskipp, Francesca, 'New Directions in Supervision' in Bayne, R., Horton, I., Bimrose, J. (eds), *New Directions in Counselling* (London: Routledge, 1996).
Inskipp, Francesca, *Skills Training* (London: Cassell, 1996).

Jacobs, Michael (ed.), *The Care Guide – A Handbook for the Caring Professions and Other Agencies* (London: Cassell, 1995).
Jones, Phil, *Drama as Therapy, Theatre as Living* (London: Routledge, 1995).
Jung, C. G., *Dreams* (London: Ark Paperbacks, 1985).

Kavanagh, Mairéad, 'The Non-Voluntary Client' in *Éisteach*, vol. 2, no. 2, Autumn 1997, Irish Association for Counselling and Therapy.
Kennedy, Patricia, 'Confidentiality and the Counselling Profession' in *Éisteach*, vol. 2, no. 2. Autumn 1997.
Kirschenbaum, H. and Henderson, V. Land (eds), *The Carl Rogers Reader* (London: Constable, 1990).

Lendrum, Susan and Syme, Gabrielle, *Gift of Tears* (London: Routledge, 1992).
Levant, R. and Shlien, J. (eds.), *The Person-Centred Approach* (New York: Praeger, 1984).

Mann, J., *Time-Limited Psychotherapy* (USA: Harvard University Press, 1973).
May, Rollo, *The Art of Counselling* (London: Condor/Souvenir Press, 1992).
McCaffrey, Anne, *The Dragons of Pern* (London: Sphere Books, 1974).

McLeod, John, 'Working with Narratives' in Bayne, R., Horton, I., Bimrose, J. (eds), *New Directions in Counselling* (London: Routledge, 1996), p. 189.

Mearns, Dave, *Developing Person-Centred Counselling* (London: Sage, 1994); *Person-Centred Counselling Training* (London: Sage, 1997).

Mearns, Dave and Thorne, Brian, *Person-Centred Counselling in Action* (London: Sage, 1988).

Merry, Tony, *Invitation to Person-Centred Psychology* (Whurr Publishers, 1997).

Molnos, A., *A Question of Time: Essentials of Brief Dynamic Therapy* (London: Karnac, 1995).


Nelson-Jones, Richard, *Effective Thinking Skills* (London: Cassell, 1989); *Practical Counselling Skills* (London: Holt, Rinehart and Winston, 1983).

Nolan, Inger, 'Imagery and Art as Symbolic Language in Psychotherapy' in *Éisteach*, vol. 1, no. 37, Summer 1996, Irish Association for Counselling and Therapy.

Noonan, Ellen and Spurling, Laurence, *The Making of a Counsellor* (Tavistock/Routledge, 1992).


O'Carroll, Austin, 'Appreciating Difference' in *Éisteach*, vol. 2, no. 5, Irish Association for Counselling and Therapy.

O'Donohue, John, *Anam Čara* (London: Transworld Publishers, 1997).

O'Farrell, Ursula, *First Steps in Counselling* (Dublin: Veritas, 1988/1998).

O'Floinn, Caoimhe, 'Women's Spirituality and Psychotherapy' in *Éisteach*, vol. 2, 8, Spring 1999.


Palmer, Stephen and Varma, Ved, (Eds.), *The Future of Counselling and Therapy* (London: Sage, 1997).

Parks, Penny, *Rescuing the Inner Child* (Souvenir Press, 1990).
Phillips, Adam, *Terrors and Experts* (Faber and Faber, 1995).

Quinn-Berger, June, 'Sand Therapy, Communication, Explanation and Individuation' in *Éisteach*, vol. 1, no. 39, Winter 1996, Irish Association for Counselling and Therapy.

Rennie, David L., *Person-Centred Counselling* (London: Sage, 1998).
Reville, William, 'Science Today', *The Irish Times*, 26 October 1998, Dublin.
Rogers, C. R., *A Way of Being*, (Boston: Houghton Mifflin, 1980); *Journal of Consulting Psychology*, vol. 21, no. 2, 1957, pp. 95-103; *On Becoming a Person* (London: Constable, 1974); *Client-Centred Therapy*, Film No. 1, in E. Shostrom (ed.), *Three Approaches to Psychotherapy*. Three 16mm colour motion pictures. (Orange, California: Psychological Films, Inc., 1965); *Client-Centred Therapy: Its Current Practice, Implications and Theory* (London: Constable, 1965); *Counselling and Psychotherapy: New Concepts in Practice* (Boston: Houghton-Mifflin, 1942).

Rogers, Kohut and Erickson, 'A Personal Perspective on Some Similarities and Differences', *Person-Centred Review* 1, (2) 1986, pp. 125-40.
Rowan, John, *Discover Your Subpersonalities* (London: Routledge, 1993).
Rycroft, Charles, *The Innocence of Dreams* (New Jersey, USA: Jason Aronson Inc., 1979/1996).

Sanders, Diana, *Counselling for Psychosomatic Problems* (London: Sage, 1996).

Sanford, Linda T., *Strong at the Broken Places* (London: Virago Press, 1990).

Seligman, M., 'The Effectiveness of Psychotherapy' in *American Psychologist* 50 (12), 1996.

Shipton, Geraldine and Smith, Eileen, *Long-Term Counselling* (London: Sage, 1998).

Spring, Jacqueline, *Cry Hard and Swim* (London: Virago, 1987).

Storr, Anthony, *The Art of Psychotherapy*, 2nd edition (United Kingdom: Butterworth/Heinemann, 1990).

Thorne, Brian, *Carl Rogers* (London: Sage, 1992); 'Counselling and Psychotherapy: The Sickness and the Prognosis' in Palmer, Stephen and Varma, Ved, (eds.), *The Future of Counselling and Therapy* (London: Sage, 1997); *Person-Centred Counselling: Therapeutic and Spiritual Dimensions* (London: Whurr Publishers, 1991); 'What are the Boundaries?' in Dryden, Windy, (ed.), *Therapists' Dilemmas* (London: Harper and Row, 1985), p. 59.

Tubridy, Áine, 'Medical and Counselling Issues in a Mind-Body Practice' in *Éisteach*, vol. 2, no. 5, Summer 1998, Irish Association for Counselling and Therapy.

Warren, Bernie (ed.), *Using the Creative Arts in Therapy* (London: Routledge, 1993)

Whitaker, Dorothy, *Using Groups to Help People* (London: Routledge, 1987).

Yalom, Irving D., 'Love's Executioner', *Penguin Psychology*, 1991.

Yeats, W. B., *The Last Romantic* (London: Arum Press, 1990).

# INDEX